HOW TO TEACH YOUR CHILD PIANO

Even If You Can't Play Yourself!

LEVEL 1

By Stephanie Parker

ISBN: 978-1-7352298-0-5

Front cover design by Adam Parker

First printing edition 2020.

parkermusicacademy.us

Table Of Contents

Introduction:

There is a false idea that in order for your child to learn to play piano you must pay hundreds of dollars each month for private instruction and piano materials. Granted, once a student reaches a certain level of achievement, then a private instructor would be necessary to continue their progress. However, **the early levels of piano can certainly be taught by any involved parent**. You do not have to have years of private lessons to do this. You do not even have to have had one private lesson to do this.

This book will make it easy to understand what your child needs to know and how to help them. YOU are your child's piano teacher. Not only are you saving literally hundreds of dollars every month, but the time you will get as you teach your child piano will build special memories that will last a lifetime.This is meant to be learned with a parent overseeing their practice to make sure they are following the techniques presented.

This book can be used from kindergarten through adulthood. The pacing will vary based on your child's age. It is recommended to not work faster than 1 lesson per week for K-5th grade. It is recommended not to work faster than 2 lessons per week for 5th grade through 9th grade. 10th grade on, it is possible to do 3 lessons a week. Once the material becomes challenging for your child to master, slow down to 1 lesson a week no matter what their age. The goal is to make this book copy in person lessons as much as possible. Set a specific day and time each week to give your child a lesson.

At each weeks lesson, your child should demonstrate, without help, the previous week lessons practice log items. If they are unable to do so, then repeat the previous weeks lesson. Repeat lessons as many times as necessary until there is a mastery of the subject material.

This book will work best when paired with the supplement theory book for this volume. The more hands on practice and repetition your child does, the easier the skills will become.

Starting each lesson - teach all the new concepts in each lesson. Before you begin teaching the next weeks lesson, you should hear all their homework from their practice log including the practice song. If any of their homework is challenging for them, that lesson should be repeated instead of moving on.

You will see something call "Parent Answer" after new songs that your child is learning. This is for the parents reference only. It is an aide to help assure you that your child is playing the song they are learning correctly. DO NOT let your child see this answer at any point in them learning the song. Children who learn piano by having the notes written in for them are not truly learning piano. Those kids end up not being able to progress beyond a certain point and become frustrated and often quit piano. If you find an in person teacher who regularly writes in most or all of the notes to your child's song....RUN!

This book is dedicated to the love of my life who is the most supportive and loving man who encouraged me to write this book. I'd also like to dedicate this book to my son, Noah, who inspired me to teach again after breaking for many years to focus on being a mom.

CHAPTER 1: LEARNING THE BASICS

LESSON 1

RIGHT HAND/LEFT HAND

Your child knowing and being able to identify their left hand versus their right hand is a basic concept that should already be learned before beginning piano. If your child is a young beginner and has not yet mastered the difference between their left hand and right hand, stop and master that skill before continuing this book.

FINGER NUMBERS

Once your child has a firm grasp on the right hand verses the left hand, it's time to teach them the finger numbers. Each finger on both hands have a number associated with them. This is extremely important to master. Initially they will learn songs that will use only their finger numbers. Eventually they will play music that will be real notes, but finger numbers will still come into play at that point all the way to the advanced levels.

Both hands have a mirrored fingering. The thumbs are 1, pointers 2, middle fingers 3, ring fingers 4, and pinky 5.

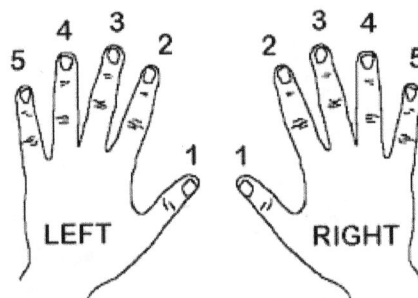

Do the following exercises with your child every day to help them get familiar with their finger numbers. Have them put both hands on the piano bench. We will talk more about hand posture later, but for now encourage them to not keep their hands flat. Instead, have the heal of the hand and finger tips only touching the bench making the hand form an arch shape (almost like the Hand is holding a tennis ball). In that position:

YOUR CHILD'S TURN TO PLAY:
* tap both hands #1 fingers
* tap both hands #2 fingers
* tap both hands #3 fingers
* tap both hands #4 fingers
* tap both hands # 5 fingers

When that becomes easy for your child mix up the hands and the finger numbers. Here is one example of many combinations of what that could look like:

YOUR CHILD'S TURN TO PLAY:
* tap RH #3 finger
* tap LH #1 finger
* tap RH #5 finger
* tap LH #2 finger
* tap RH # 4 finger

Part of learning to play the piano is to practice 3-6 days every week. Get a notebook and make a practice list for your child to follow during their practice time. These finger exercises should be the first thing on your practice list to work on daily.

UP/DOWN THE KEYS

When learning to play the piano the ideal instrument is an actual piano. I understand that is not always feasible when just starting lessons. If you need to start on a keyboard, you want to make sure it has 88 keys and those keys are weighted.

Identify on either your piano or keyboard the middle of your piano. On a keyboard you need to count to the middle of the 88 keys. On the piano you will see words above the keys that label what brand piano you are playing. That is the location of the middle of the piano.

When we refer to going up the piano it means starting at the middle and heading to the right as demonstrated by the image below.

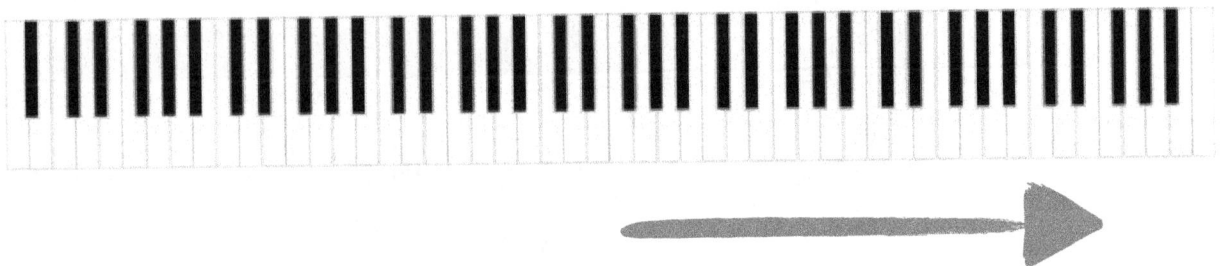

YOUR CHILD'S TURN TO PLAY:

* Start at the middle and play random notes going up the keys. Do you hear how they sound thinner the higher they go? Almost like a balloon going higher and higher into the air.

When we refer to going down the piano it means starting at the middle and heading to the left of the piano as demonstrated by the image below.

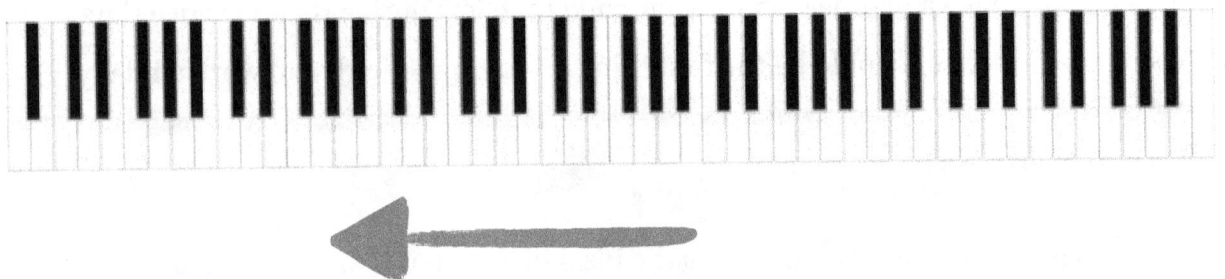

YOUR CHILD'S TURN TO PLAY:

* Start at the middle and play random notes going down the keys. Do you hear how they sound deeper the lower you go? Almost like a bear going deeper and deeper into a cave.

GROUPS OF 3 BLACK NOTES/GROUPS OF 2

Look at the black notes on your piano. Do you see how they are in groups of 2 and in groups of 3? This is very important to be able to easily identify the groups of 2 and 3 black notes

Image below: The Red Circle is a group of 2 and the blue circle is a group of 3

YOUR CHILD'S TURN TO PLAY:
   * Play all the groups of 2 black notes on the piano
   * Play all the groups of 3 black notes on the piano

Daily Practice Log:

   * *Finger exercises*
   * *Notes going up the piano*
   * *Notes going down the piano*
   * *Play all the groups of 2 black notes on the piano*
   * *Play all the groups of 3 black notes on the piano*
   * *Corresponding Theory Chapter*

NOTE TO PARENTS: At the end of each lesson is the practice log. Have your child practice each item on the practice log every day 3-6 days a week for 5-10 minute a day. Practice times will increase as the student advances, but in the beginning start with small achievable goals as you are making regular piano practice a habit. DO NOT continue to the next lesson until this lesson practice log is able to be done correctly and independently of parental guidance.

Create a chart like the image below in your Childs piano folder. Each week write down your Childs homework and have them check off that they have practiced their homework as demonstrated in the image. Part of your job as their teacher is to teach them to practice efficiently. Go over their completed homework chart at each lesson and talk about any checkmarks that are missing and how to improve on practice in the following week.

	Day 1	Day 2	Day 3	Day 4
Finger exercises	✓			
Notes going up the piano	✓			
Notes going down the piano	✓			
Play all groups of 2 black notes	✓			
Play all groups of 3 black notes	✓			
Corresponding theory chapter	✓			

LESSON 2

FINDING C'S ON THE PIANO

Do you remember how you taught your child to find the groups of 2 and 3 black notes on the piano? We are going to put that knowledge to use now to learn how to find the note C on the piano.

Whatever you do, DO NOT write the note names on the piano/keyboard. It is absolutely essential that your child learns to find and identify the notes on their own. As you search for a piano teacher down the road, if you find a teacher that recommends writing in the notes on the keys....Run.

To Find C:

1) Have your child find the groups of 2 black notes.

2) Have them find the lower of the first black note in that group of two black notes

3) Now have them go DOWN to the white note right before that 1st black note. That note is C.

How to Find 'C' Notes

'C' is the white note immediately to the left of the group of 2 black notes

This note is also 'C,' but sounds different because you're playing it in a different spot

YOUR CHILD'S TURN TO PLAY:

* Have them play all the C's on the piano

(NOTE: be careful that they only do this on the group of 2 black notes. If they choose the white note before the group of 3 black notes that is not a C)

QUARTER NOTES

Soon we will begin reading music and your child will need to know how long to hold each note. The different amount of time we hold a note is called different rhythms.

The image below is called a quarter note. A quarter note is worth 1 beat which means we hold it just for the count of 1.

QUARTER NOTE - ♩

YOUR CHILD'S TURN TO PLAY:

* Have your child Clap and count aloud 1 for each quarter note below

♩   ♩   ♩   ♩

HALF NOTES

The image below is called a half note. A Half note is worth 2 beats which means we hold it while we count both 1 AND 2.

HALF NOTE - ♩

YOUR CHILD'S TURN TO PLAY:

* Have your child Clap and count aloud 1-2 for each half note shown

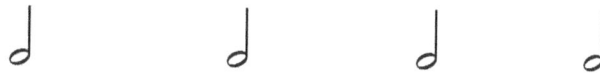

♩   ♩   ♩   ♩

(NOTE: You do not clap 2x on the half note. Instead you hold your single clap while you say 1-2)

YOUR CHILD'S TURN TO PLAY:

* Have your child clap and count aloud either 1 or 1-2 for each quarter and half note shown.

♩   ♩   ♩   ♩   ♩   ♩

WHOLE NOTES

The image below is called a whole note. A whole note is worth 4 beats which means we hold it while we count 1 - 2- 3 - 4

WHOLE NOTE - 𝗢

YOUR CHILD'S TURN TO PLAY:

* Have your child Clap and count aloud 1-2-3-4 for each whole note shown

(NOTE: You do not clap 4x on the whole note. Instead you hold your single clap while you say 1-2-3-4)

𝅝   𝅝   𝅝

* Have your child clap and count aloud either 1 or 1-2 or 1 -2 - 3- 4 for each quarter, half, and whole note shown.

♩   ♩   𝅗𝅥   𝅝   ♩   ♩   𝅗𝅥   𝅝

MAKING FLASHCARDS

Now that we have learned the terms quarter note, half note, whole note it is time to make flashcards for these terms. Copy the images of the quarter note, half note, and whole note onto the front of three separate flashcards and put the definition of both their name and how many beats they receive on the back of the flashcard. Quiz your child on these terms daily. We will be regularly adding more terms to your flashcard pile.

PIANO POSTURE

Soon we will be playing music on the piano. When that time comes I will occasionally remind you to check your child's posture. Even when I'm not reminding you, you should always be checking for proper posture.

Bench seating: Your child should be closer to the front edge or middle of the bench. Their bottom should never be all the way to the back of the bench.

Bench position: Your child needs to not have the bench too close to the piano. Their knees should just barely be under the keyboard.

Feet position: Feet should be straight out in front of you with feet flat on the floor. If your child is too small to reach the floor I suggest a step stool until they can.

Sitting position: Back should be completely straight with shoulders back and relaxed.

Elbow position: It is common for students to stick their elbows out when trying to reach notes. Elbows should be next to the body at all times

Hand position: Possibly the most important aspect for you to check at each and every days lesson AND practice is your Child's hand position. Arms and wrists should be level with the keys with fingers curved so that all the notes are being played with the fleshy pad of the finger right above the nail.

Finger nails: To achieve proper hand position, finger nails should be kept trimmed at all times.

YOUR CHILD'S TURN TO PLAY:

* Have your child practice sitting at the piano getting used to the proper piano posture

Daily Practice Log:

    * Finger exercises

    *Notes going up the piano

    *Notes going down the piano

    *Finding all the C's on the piano

    * Flashcard terms

    * Practice Piano posture

    *Corresponding Theory Chapter

DO NOT continue to the next lesson until this chapters practice log is able to be done with relative ease even if it takes longer than the recommended 3-6 days of practice 5 - 10 minutes a day.

LESSON 3

FINDING ALL THE NOTES ON THE PIANO

Review with your child how to find the C's on the piano. If this is challenging at all for your child do not continue until they understand this concept.

When teaching your child the notes of the piano it is much easier to start at note C than to start at A like they might in school for the alphabet. The piano keys follow the alphabet, but it ends at the letter G at which point it starts back over at the beginning of the alphabet with letter A. So starting at C the note order would be C - D - E - F - G - A - B.

YOUR CHILD'S TURN TO PLAY:

*Have your child play a C on the piano. Then have them play the next white note up. Thats a D

*Have them play the next white note up which is E

*Then have them play the next white note which is F

*Then have them play the next white note which is G

*Then have them play the next white note which is A

*Then have them play the next white note which is B

*The next white note should be another C. That is all the notes of the piano. It follows the alphabet from A-G.

Emphasize with your child that once they reach the note G that is the end of the musical alphabet and it starts over at A at that point.

YOUR CHILD'S TURN TO PLAY:
* Have your child play all the white notes in order going UP the piano and saying their names out loud.

FORTE

Our next term to add to our flashcards is Forte. It means to play loudly. On the front of the flashcard copy the image below. On the back write forte (loud).

Forte - f

PIANO

Our next term to add to our flashcards is piano. It means to play softly. On the front of the flashcard copy the image below. On the back write piano (soft).

Piano - p

STEPPING UP THE KEYS

Review with your child going up the keyboard. The music they will be reading looks like it is going up the page if they want you to go up the keyboard. It looks almost like steps up a mountain. This means to start on the note indicated and play each of the very next white notes.

YOUR CHILD'S TURN TO PLAY:

C NOTE on
Right Hand
1 finger

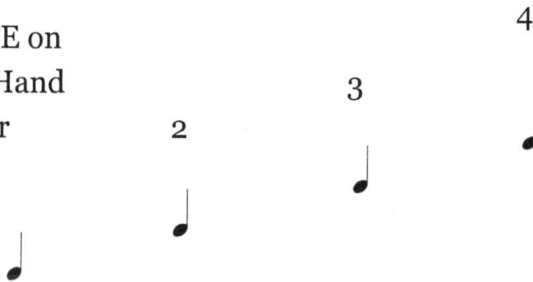

2

3

4

In the example above, place your right hand on the piano with your 1 finger on C
(Remember the 1 finger is the thumb). Notice how each note looks like it's one step up
the "mountain" higher than the last. That means to have your child play 'C' then step up
to each next white note like the music.

(The answer would be they should have played C - D - E - F.)

PRACTICE SONG lesson 3: (EACH 1 FINGER SHOULD BE NOTE C)

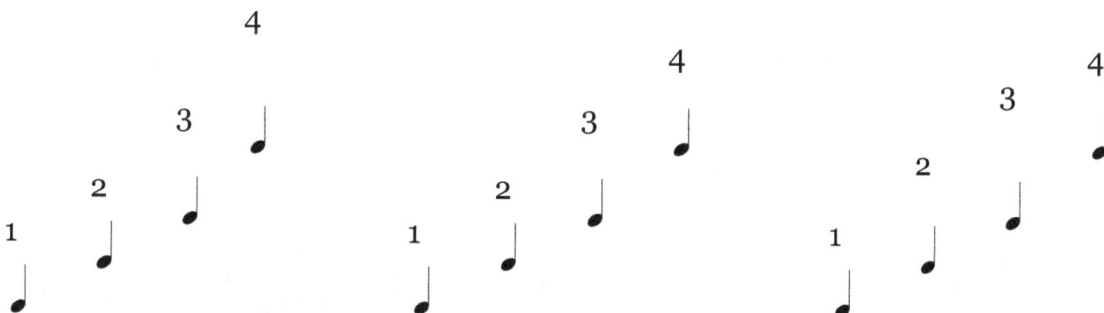

1   2   3   4   1   2   3   4   1   2   3   4

Daily Practice Log:

    * Finger exercises

    *Notes going up the piano

    *Notes going down the piano

    *Finding all the C's on the piano

    * Finding notes on the piano C - D - E - F - G - A - B

    *Flashcard terms

    *Practice Piano posture

    * Practice song

    *Corresponding Theory Chapter

(PARENT NOTE: practice should now be closer to 10 minutes each day to accommodate playing their practice song 2-3 times a day as well as all the other items on the practice log)

DO NOT continue to the next lesson until this chapters practice log is able to be done with relative ease even if it takes longer than the recommended 3-6 days of practice 5 - 10 minutes a day.

IMPORTANT: From here on out I will provide a parent answer for your child's practice song. It is extremely important that at no time does your child see or reference this answer. It is to help you as the teacher only.

(Practice song answer for parents: *C - D - E - F,*

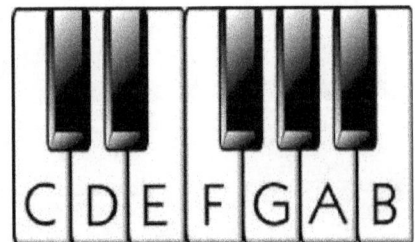

                                     C - D - E - F,

                                     C - D - E- F)

LESSON 4

FINDING THE NOTES ON THE PIANO IN RANDOM ORDER

Review with your child the names of the keys. Then have your child independently play and name each white note going up the piano until the reach the next C.

Songs will not always start with C so it's important to be able to find any note on the piano. Teach your child to think of C as a sort of home-base. Whatever note they may be looking for, start at C and count up to the note they are looking for.

YOUR CHILD'S TURN TO PLAY:

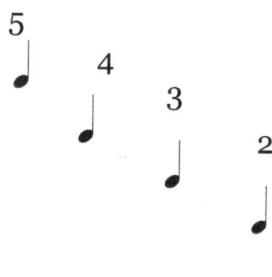

* Once they can play and name the piano notes in order Call out a random order of notes and have them play the notes.
* One example is: (Each time you do this exercise change the order)

C - G - D - A - E - B - F

STEPPING DOWN THE KEYS

Review with your child what it means to go down the keyboard. Just like going up the keyboard, the music they are reading looks like it is going down the page if they want you step down on the keys.

YOUR CHILD'S TURN TO PLAY:

5
4
3
2
1

(C NOTE on Right Hand **1** finger)

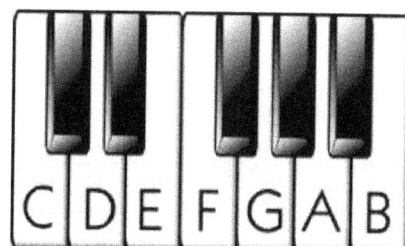

C D E F G A B

In the previous example, place your right hand on the piano with your 1 finger on C. This time the song will start on our 5 finger, the pinky, which should be on a G note. Notice how each note looks like it is one step down the "mountain." That means have your child play their 5 finger then step down to each next white note like the music. (*Answer for parents: your child should have played G - F- E - D - C*)

FINGER NUMBERS

You have taught your child finger numbers and hopefully they are pretty familiar with it at this point. Now you will start to see finger numbers in your child's music.

We have gone over how the music can move up and down like mountain steps. Teach your child using the example below that it is not always straight up and down the mountain. Sometimes it goes back and forth in smaller segments. To help your child acclimate to this you will see finger numbers above each note, for now, to help them know what to play. Remember right hand 1 should be on C.

YOUR CHILD'S TURN TO PLAY:

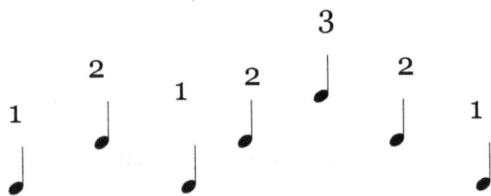

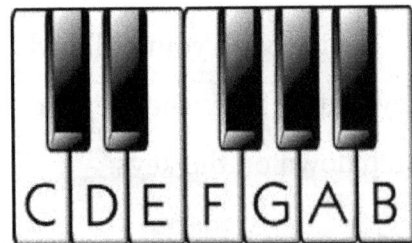

(*Answer for parents: C - D - C - D - E - D - C*)

PRACTICE SONG Lesson 4:
(EACH 1 FINGER SHOULD BE NOTE C)

Daily Practice Log:

    *Finding all the C's on the piano

    * Finding notes on the piano C - D - E - F - G - A - B

    * Flashcard terms

    * Practice Piano posture

    * Practice song

    Corresponding Theory Chapter

(Parent answer: C - D - E - D - C - D - E - F - E - D - C)

(PARENT NOTE: Finger exercises and going up and down the piano has been taken off the practice log. It is assumed at this point that your child has mastered these skills. If that is not the case pause all lessons until those skills are mastered.)

DO NOT continue to the next lesson until this chapters practice log is able to be done with relative ease even if it takes longer than the recommended 3-6 days of practice 5 - 10 minutes a day.

LESSON 5

<u>CURVED FINGERS</u>

In the very beginning of this book I talked of proper hand posture. Now that we are starting to play songs I want to remind you how to practically apply this. As your child is playing these songs check their sitting posture. Most importantly, every time they play a note make sure their wrist is level with their arm, their hand is making an arch (their fingers are NOT flat on the keys) and that each note they play is played with the fleshy pad above their nail.

This is the CORRECT way to curve fingers

This is the WRONG way to curve fingers. Do not allow the first joint to collapse.

YOUR CHILD'S TURN TO PLAY:

*Have your child place their hands on the piano (RH 1 finger on C) with curved fingers and play finger 1 - 2 - 3 - 4 - 5 without letting joint collapse.

NOTES STAYING THE SAME

We have reviewed notes climbing up and down the mountain. Now it is time to teach your child how to recognize notes that stay the same. When a note right next to the note before it looks to be in the same exact location that means to play the same note again. When that happens you will not see the same finger number repeated. It is understood that you keep using the same finger number. Here is an example.

YOUR CHILD'S TURN TO PLAY:

Parent: show your child how the finger number was shown for the the first note, but not for any subsequent note that stayed the same.

(Parent answer C - C - D - D - E - E)

PRACTICE SONG Lesson 5:
(RIGHT HAND 1 FINGER SHOULD BE ON NOTE C)

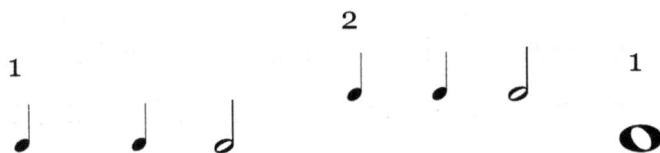

Daily Practice Log:

    * Finding notes on the piano in this order: F - D - B - E - A - C - G

    * Flashcard terms

    * Practice Piano posture

    * Practice song

    *Corresponding Theory Chapter

(Parent answer: C - C - C - D - D - D - C... Don't forget to make sure your child holds the half notes for 2 counts and the whole note for 4 counts.)

(PARENT NOTE: Finding all the C's has been taken off the practice log. It is assumed at this point that your child has mastered this skill. If that is not the case pause all lessons until that skill is mastered.)

DO NOT continue to the next lesson until this chapters practice log is able to be done with relative ease even if it takes longer than the recommended 3-6 days of practice 5 - 10 minutes a day.

LESSON 6

<u>FINDING MIDDLE C</u>

Your child is now able to find All the C's on the piano with ease. This means it is time to teach him/her how to find "middle C" because middle C is a very important note.

To find middle C look for the words in the middle of your piano that identify what type of piano you own. The C directly below those words is middle C. **In all the songs we will learn for this level 1 book the right hand number 1 finger will be placed on middle C.**

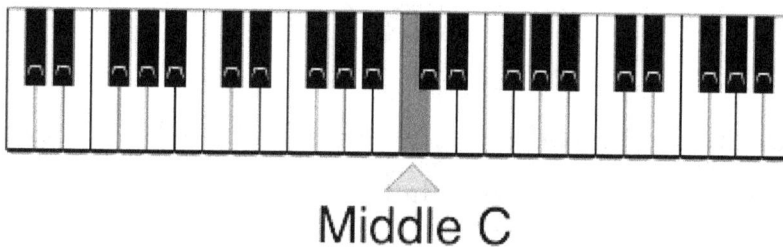

Middle C

YOUR CHILD'S TURN TO PLAY:

*Have your child alternate from playing all the C's on the piano to identifying middle C. Do this multiple times.

<u>LEFT HAND LOCATION</u>

Now that you know the specific 'C' to place your child's right hand on, you can identify where to place their left hand.

(On this image, the left hand location should be the shaded C below middle C)

Middle C

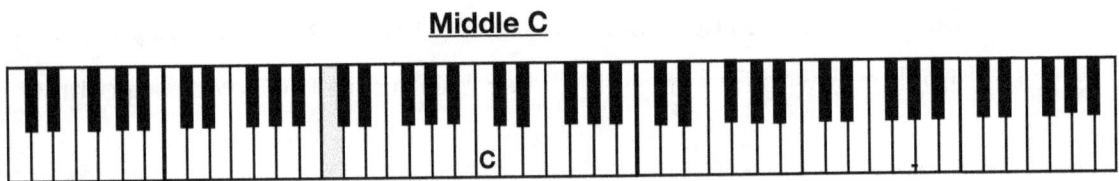

YOUR CHILD'S TURN TO PLAY:

* Have your child find the C below middle C.

* Have your child place their Left hand 5 finger on that C

This is the location the left hand will play for all of this books level 1 songs: 5 finger (pinky) on the C below middle C.

PLAYING SONGS WITH THE LEFT HAND

All the concepts of following the finger numbers as the notes step up, down and stay the same apply to the left hand just as they do to the right. The main difference you will see as you teach your child to play with their left hand is a different order of finger notes. For now, will begin with the 5 finger in the left hand; whereas, the right hand will begin with the 1 finger.

The left hand is weaker for the majority of children as it is their non dominant hand. Please pay even closer attention when the left hand is playing to look for curved fingers.

PRACTICE SONG Lesson 6:
To be played with the left hand(EACH 5 FINGER SHOULD BE NOTE C)

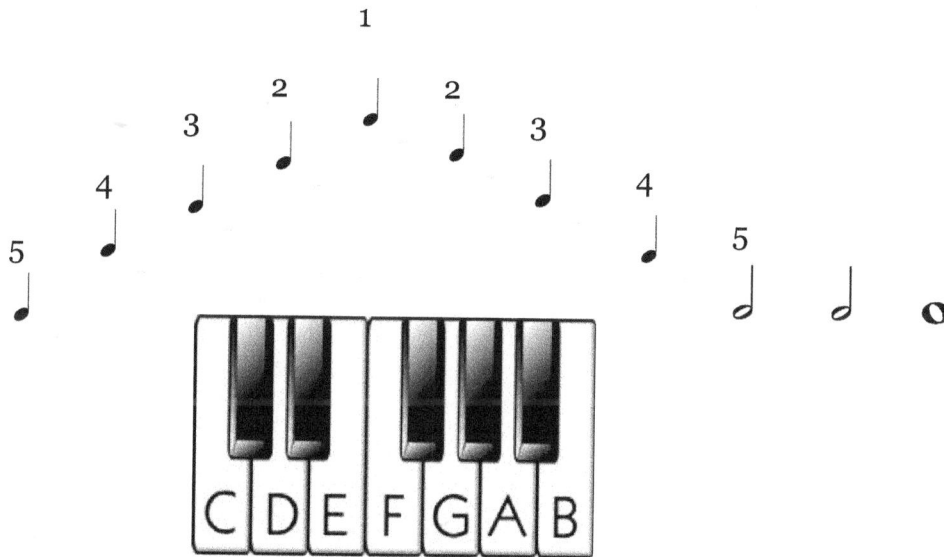

Daily Practice Log:

* *Finding notes on the piano in the order: F - D - B - E - A - C - G*

* *Flashcard terms*

* *Practice song*

*Corresponding Theory Chapter

(*Parent answer: C - D -E - F - G -F - E - D - C - C - C.. make sure the pinky and all fingers stay curved)*

DO NOT continue to the next lesson until this lesson's practice log is able to be done with relative ease. Your child should be able to complete the entire practice log at their next weeks lesson completely independently in order to move on. If they can't move on, repeat last weeks lesson

CHAPTER 2: LINES, SPACING AND COUNTING MUSIC

LESSON 1

STAFF

Our next term to add to our flashcards is staff. It has 5 lines and 4 spaces in-between the lines. The staff is where the notes are placed and is how we read music.

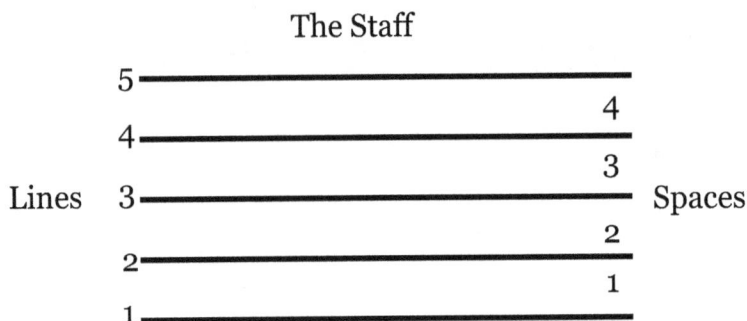

The Staff

Lines

Spaces

5
4
3
2
1

4
3
2
1

On the front of the flashcard copy the image below. On the back simply write staff.

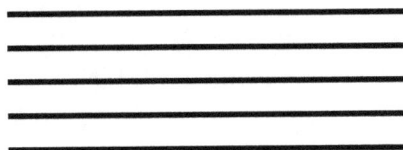

TREBLE CLEF

Our next term to add to our flashcards is Treble clef. It is a symbol at the begging of each line of music. In this level, anytime you see the treble clef it means you are to play the music with your RIGHT hand. On the front of the flashcard copy the image to the right. On the back write treble clef-RH. In ( ) write G clef on the back of the flashcard. Don't make your child learn the term G clef at this point. Once, they master the term treble clef add the alternate name of the symbol G clef.

PRACTICE SONG lesson 1:

To be played with the left hand 5 on C

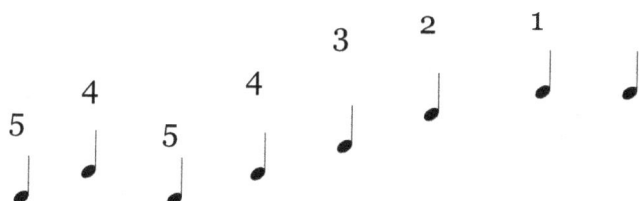

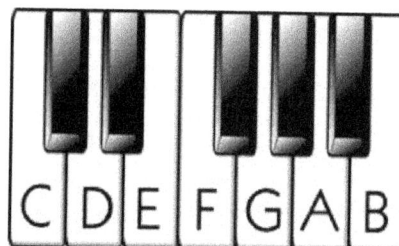

Daily Practice Log (3-6 days @ 5-10 minutes each day):

    * Finding notes on the piano F - D - B - E - A - C - G

    * Flashcard terms

    * Practice song

    *Corresponding Theory Chapter

(*Parent Answer: C - D - C - D - E - F - G - G)*

DO NOT continue to the next lesson until this lesson's practice log is able to be done with relative ease. Your child should be able to complete the entire practice log at their next weeks lesson completely independently in order to move on. If they can't move on, repeat last weeks lesson

LESSON 2

BASS CLEF

Our next term to add to our flashcards is bass clef. Bass clef is a symbol at the begging of each line of music. In this level, anytime you see the bass clef it means you are to play the music with your LEFT hand. On the front of the flashcard, copy the image to the right. On the back write bass clef-LH. In ( ) write F clef. Don't make your child learn the F clef term at this point. Once they master the bass clef term, then they can learn the alternate name of F clef at that point.

LINES ON THE STAFF

The image below shows an example of line notes. Those circles are called note heads and when a note head is placed directly on the line, with the line cutting it down the middle, it means that it is called a line note.

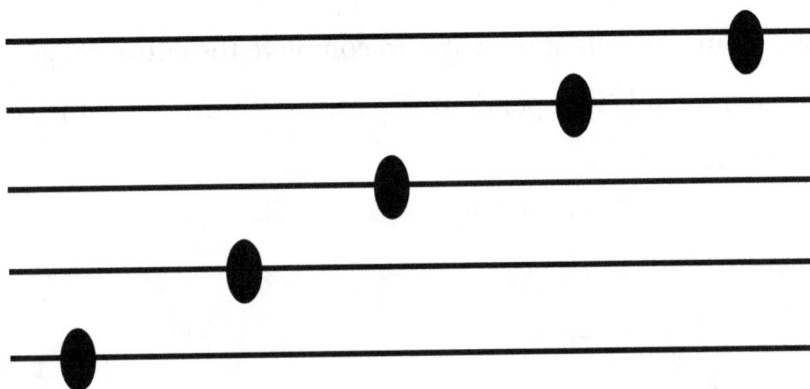

PRACTICE SONG lesson 2: To be played with the right hand 1 on middle C

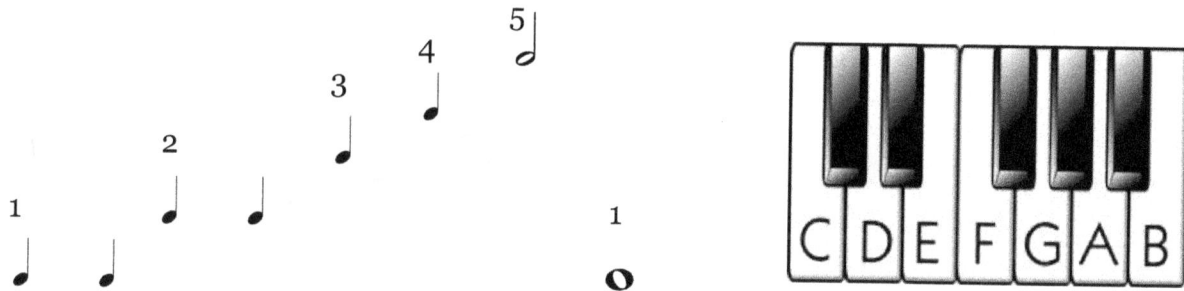

Daily Practice Log (3-6 days @ 5-10 minutes each day):

　* Finding notes on the piano F - D - B - E - A - C - G

　* Flashcard terms

　* Practice song

　*Corresponding Theory Chapter

(Parent Answer: C - C - D - D - E - F - G - C. Make sure the half note and whole note get held the proper number of beats)

DO NOT continue to the next lesson until this lesson's practice log is able to be done with relative ease. Your child should be able to complete the entire practice log at their next weeks lesson completely independently in order to move on. If they can't move on, repeat last weeks lesson

LESSON 3

BAR LINE

Our next term to add to the flashcards is Bar Line. A bar line is a vertical line on a staff to divide the music. On the front of the flashcard draw the image in example 1. On the back of the flashcard write bar line.

Example 1: A single bar line

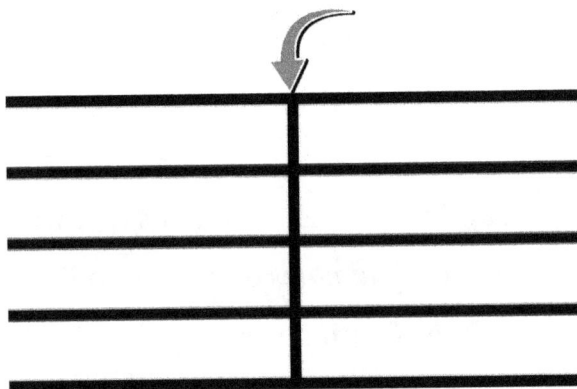

Example 2: Here you will notice many bar lines

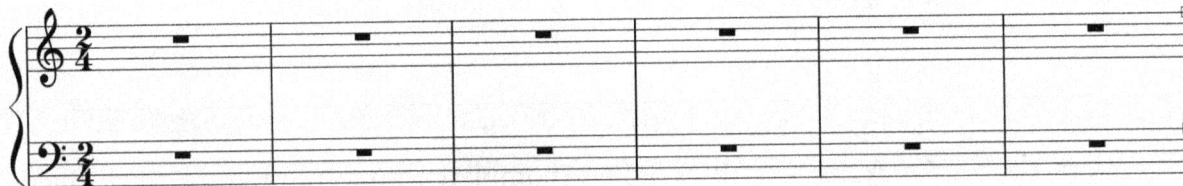

SPACES ON THE STAFF

The image below shows an example of space notes. The circle note heads, when placed directly between the lines, is called a space note.

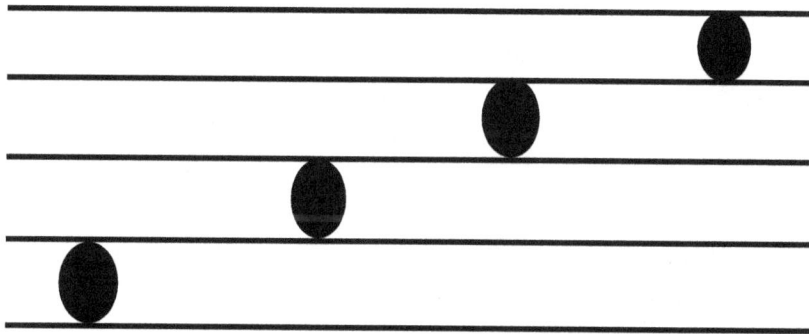

PRACTICE SONG lesson 3: To be played with the right hand 1 on middle C

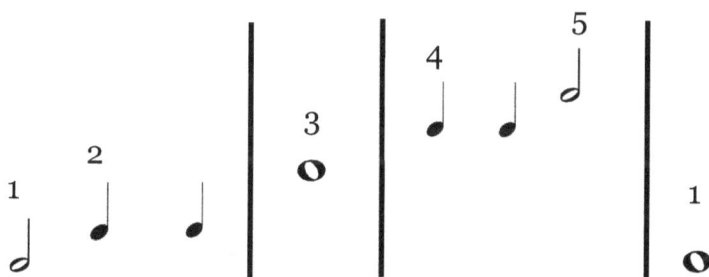

Daily Practice Log (3-6 days @ 5-10 minutes each day):

    * Finding notes on the piano F - B - D - E - C - A - G

    * Flashcard terms

    * Practice song

    *Corresponding Theory Chapter

(Parent Answer: C - D - D - E - F - F - G - C. Make sure the half note and whole note get held. Point out the bar lines to your child)

DO NOT continue to the next lesson until this lesson's practice log is able to be done with relative ease. Your child should be able to complete the entire practice log at their next weeks lesson completely independently in order to move on. If they can't move on, repeat last weeks lesson

LESSON 4

<u>MEASURE</u>

Our next term to add to the flashcards is measure. A measure is a section on the staff that comes between two bar lines. On the front of the flashcard draw the image below. On the back of the flashcard write measure.

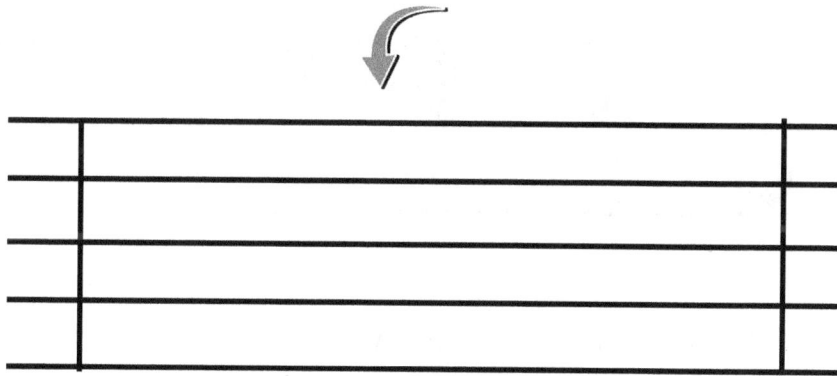

It might help to draw on the back of the flash card the image below as a guide to understanding the terms your child is memorizing.

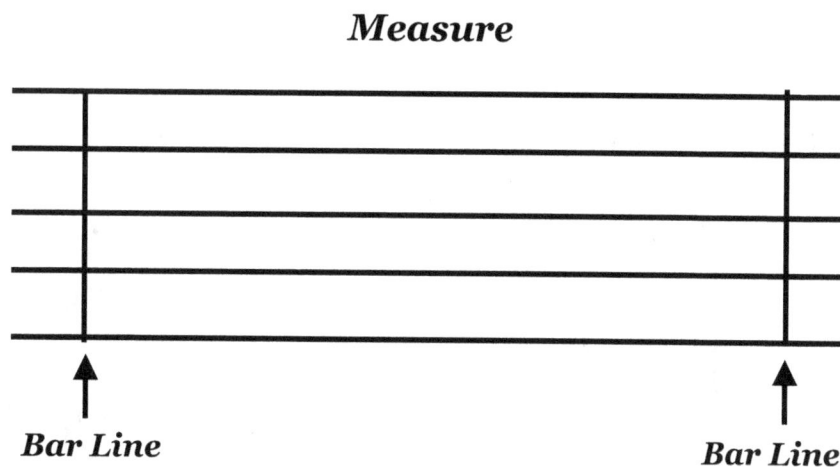

Measure

Bar Line   **Bar Line**

LINES VS SPACES

Notice how on the example below the notes alternate between line and space notes.

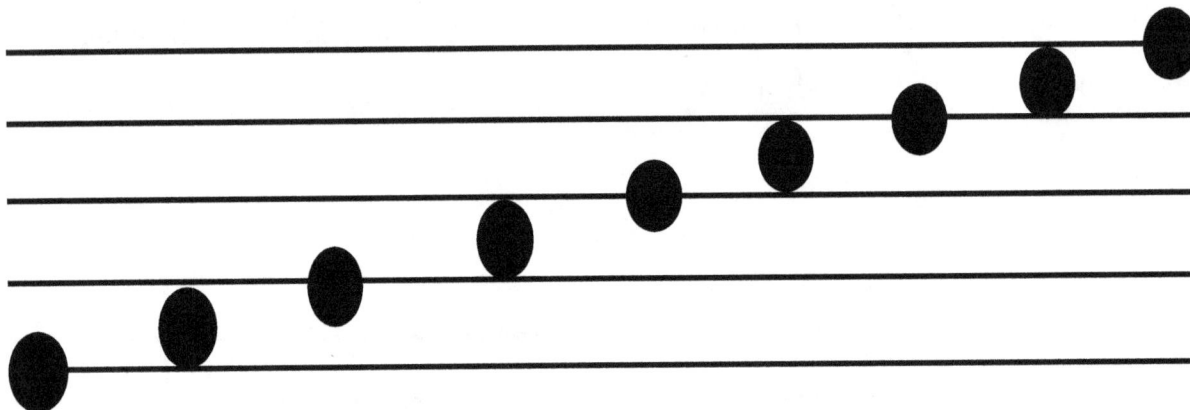

YOUR CHILD'S TURN TO PLAY:

*Point in order to the notes on the image above and have your child identify if it is a line note or space note. They should answer line, space, line, space etc.

*Point in random order to the notes in the image above. Have your child identify if it is a line note or space note.

PRACTICE SONG lesson 4: To be played with the right hand 1 on middle C

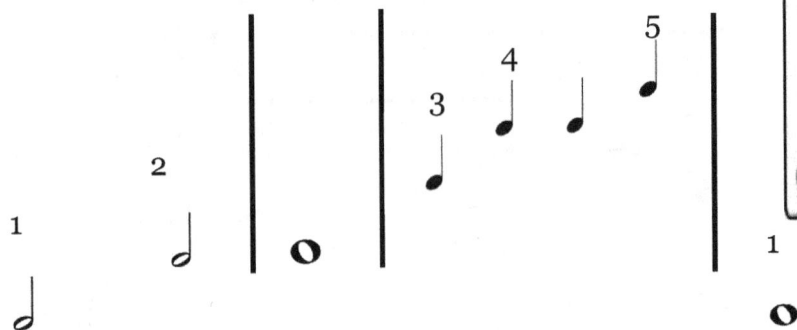

Daily Practice Log (3-6 days @ 5-10 minutes each day):

*   * Finding notes on the piano F - B - A - E - C - G - D*

*   * Flashcard terms*

*   * Practice song*

*   *Corresponding Theory Chapter*

(*Parent Answer: C - D - D - E - F - F - G - C. Make sure the half note and whole note get held. Point out the bar lines to your child)*

DO NOT continue to the next lesson until this lesson's practice log is able to be done with relative ease. Your child should be able to complete the entire practice log at their next weeks lesson completely independently in order to move on. If they can't move on, repeat last weeks lesson

LESSON 5

DOUBLE BAR LINE

Our next term to add to the flashcards is Double Bar Line. A double bar line is two vertical lines. At this level, it will always mean you have reached the end of the song. On the front of the flashcard draw the image below. On the back of the flashcard write Double Bar line - we've reached the end.

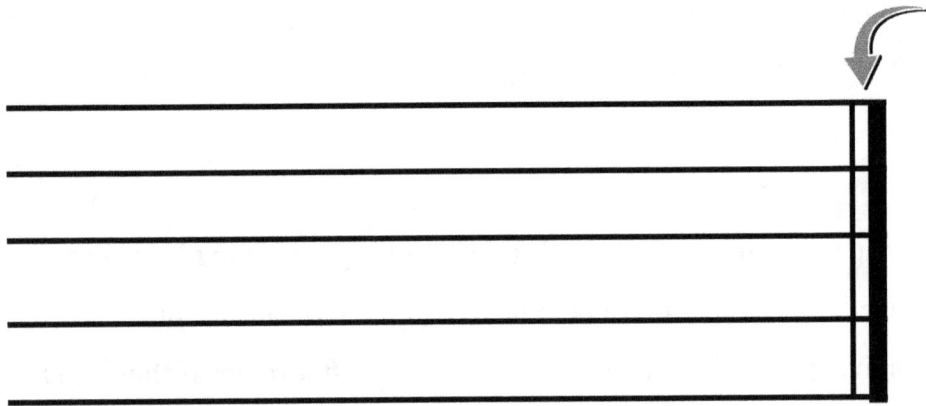

COUNTING MUSIC

At this point in our lessons, every measure needs to count 1-2-3-4. Think of the bar line as an eraser line. When you see the bar line the counts grease and you start over at 1 again at the beginning of the next measure.

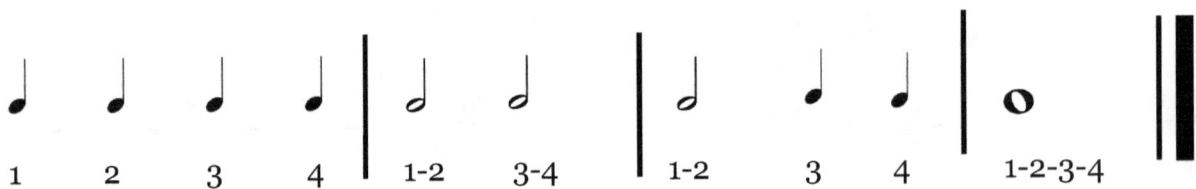

YOUR CHILD'S TURN TO PLAY:

* Have your child clap the rhythm above and count aloud while clapping.

PRACTICE SONG lesson 5: To be played with the right hand 1 on middle C

Daily Practice Log (3-6 days @ 5-10 minutes each day)::
  * * Finding notes on the piano*
    F - D - A - E - C - G - B
  * * Flashcard terms*
  * * Practice song*
  * *Corresponding Theory Chapter*

(Parent Answer: C for all the notes. The notes are easier in this song so your child can practice counting to 4 in each measure while playing the C note)

DO NOT continue to the next lesson until this lesson's practice log is able to be done with relative ease. Your child should be able to complete the entire practice log at their next weeks lesson completely independently in order to move on. If they can't move on, repeat last weeks lesson

LESSON 6

DOTTED HALF NOTE

Our next term to add to our flashcards is the dotted half note. It looks just like the half note except it has a dot to the RIGHT of it. When you see a dotted half note it is worth 3 beats. On the front of the flashcard draw the image below. On the back of the flashcard write dotted half note - worth 3 beats.

C POSITION

We will be referring to C position every lesson from this point out. C position refers to the right hand 1 finger (thumb) on middle C and the left hand 5 finger (pinky) on the C below middle C.

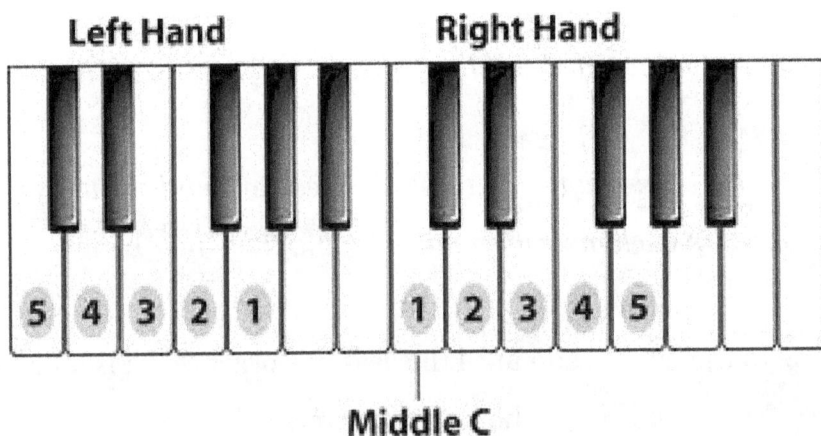

YOUR CHILD'S TURN TO PLAY:

* Have your child place their hands in C position

PRACTICE SONG lesson 6: To be played by both hands. First line plays with the right hand. Then the second line plays with the left hand. Place both hands in C position for the duration of the entire song. Do not let your child rest the hand that isn't playing in their lap. It stays on the piano.

RIGHT HAND:

LEFT HAND:

Daily Practice Log (3-6 days @ 5-10 minutes each day):

    * Finding notes on the piano F - D - A - E - C - G - B

    * Flashcard terms

    * Practice song

    *Corresponding Theory Chapter

(Parent Answer: RH: C - C - D -E - F - G - G- G - G - C

          LH: C - C - D -E - F - G - G- G - G - C

DO NOT continue to the next lesson until this lesson's practice log is able to be done with relative ease. Your child should be able to complete the entire practice log at their next weeks lesson completely independently in order to move on. If they can't move on, repeat last weeks lesson

CHAPTER 3: READING MUSIC ON THE TREBLE CLEF

LESSON 1

MEZZO FORTE

Our next term we will add to the flashcards is Mezzo Forte. Mezzo Forte means medium loud. The abbreviation of this term is *mf*. On the front of the flashcard write *mf* and on the back of the flash card write mezzo forte - medium loud. (note: when teaching this, mezzo is pronounced *met-zo)*

TREBLE CLEF: READING SPACE NOTES

Your child is ready to begin learning to recognize actual piano notes. We will start with the space notes. Starting from the bottom space up to the top of space spells the word F - A - C - E. Each space standing for one letter of that word.

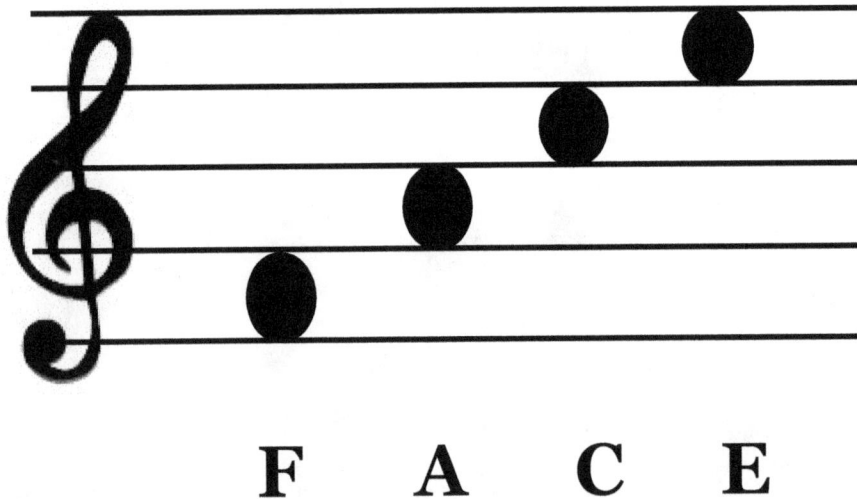

F   A   C   E

MAKING NOTE FLASHCARDS

You have been making flashcards for all the terms your child has learned and they have been studying those terms each week. Now it is time to make a separate batch of flashcards for the notes they are learning. The image below will show you what your flashcards should look like thus far. You can also find a website and print flashcards; however, I recommend if you do that to separate out only the ones that we have learned this far and add as you go. (*For all future notes we learn, please follow this same format for creating flashcards*)

On the front draw this image and on the back write F.

On the front draw this image and on the back write A.

On the front draw this image and on the back write C.

On the front draw this image and on the back write E.

PRACTICE SONG Lesson 1: To be played by both hands SIMULTANEOUSLY. Top line the right hand bottom line the left hand. Place both hands in C position for the duration of the entire song.

RIGHT HAND:

LEFT HAND:

Daily Practice Log (4-6 days @ 10-15 minutes each day):

    * Flashcards for terms

    * Flashcards for notes

    * Practice song

    *Corresponding Theory Chapter

(Parent Answer:Music is to be read left hand and right hand at the same time from left to right. So in this song the right hand plays C - D - E then the Left hand plays C - D - E, then the Right hand plays C - C - C, then the Left hand plays C - C - C)

PARENT NOTE: Your child should be accustomed now to 3-6 days of practice each week for 5-10 minutes a day after doing It for 12 lessons. **It is time to increase their practice time 4-6 days each week for 10-15 minutes a day.**

Repeat last weeks lesson if your child cannot complete its' entire practice log independently.

LESSON 2

STARTING LESSONS WITH FLASHCARDS

At this point it is important your child has been studying their flashcards during each days practice time. It is time to add flashcards to your routine as teacher during each lesson you give them.

From this point out, make sure all note and term flashcards that we have learned to date are gone over at each lesson. This is so you can see where your child is struggling with the flashcards and guide them in their practice time how best to study the cards so they master them all.

As we increase the number of cards, especially note flashcards, many young children become overwhelmed doing them all in one sitting. For those kids, I break them up and do half the flashcards in the beginning of the lesson/practice time and the other half at the end of the lesson/practice time.

Mastering the note flashcards is absolutely one of the most important parts of learning to play the piano. Make sure to make it a priority in both lessons and especially their practice time.

READING MIDDLE C AND D

For the first notes you have taught your child, F - A - C - E, there was a fun saying to remember it. The next two notes do not have a fun saying. They need to be just memorized, but these next two notes are the most important notes as we will be using them the most at this level, so make sure to spend the proper time mastering these memory notes.

The notes are Middle C and D. Make sure to point out to your child that both of these notes hang below the staff. The C hangs far below the staff with a line through it. It is a line note. The D hangs right below the staff with no line though it making it a space note.

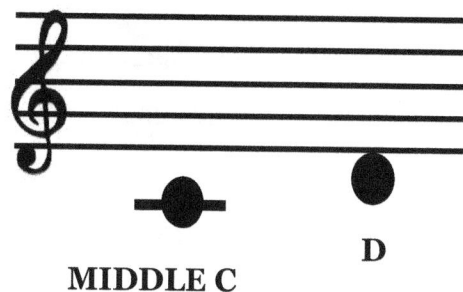

MIDDLE C

D

Please make two separate flashcards for the two notes above in the same format that we made the previous flashcards.

PRACTICE SONG Lesson 2: To be played by both hands Simultaneously. Top line the right hand bottom line the left hand. Place both hands in C position for the duration of the entire song.

RIGHT HAND:

1 2 3 4 5

LEFT

1 2 3 4 5

Daily Practice Log (4-6 days @ 10-15 minutes each day):

* *Flashcards for terms*

* *Flashcards for notes*

* *Practice song*

Corresponding Theory Chapter

(Parent Answer: Music is to be read left hand and right hand at the same time from left to right. So in this song the right hand plays C - C - D - D - E - F - G then the Left hand plays, G - G - F - F - E - D - C.... Notice the left hand is in the C position, but doesn't begin on C it begins on G)

Repeat last weeks lesson if your child cannot complete its' entire practice log independently.

LESSON 3

<u>C SCALE GOING UP RH</u>

It is important to learn scales when learning to play piano. When you eventually find an in person teacher, make sure to look for a teacher that incorporates scales.

The reason scales are important is because not only does it help you understand how music works, but it also refines the student's technique. Scales are an opportunity to practice with a focused intensity on curved fingers, proper body and arm posture, and many other aspects we will cover as we progress. To start we will learn only the right hand and only have the scale go up.

Place your child's right hand in C position. They will be playing every single white note from C to C, but with a specific fingering.

It is especially important before beginning that your child has proper hand posture. The hand should be arched (looking like a 'C' shape) with curved fingers.

First, they will play C - D - E with the fingers 1 - 2 - 3. This is the tricky part. As they're holding the 3rd finger down on E, the thumb will go underneath fingers 2 and 3 to play the next note: F. I tell the students their hand is a tunnel and the thumb, 1 finger, is going through the tunnel to the next note. (Dont let them twist their arm to reach the F)

Once they go through the tunnel to play the F note with the 1 finger immediately let go of the E note and shift the whole hand so your hand is in line with the new position of the thumb so it can play the remainder of the notes.

So the final notes are F - G - A - B - C played with fingers 1 - 2- 3- 4- 5.

Now that we have begun scales, make sure each of your child's practice days and lessons begins with scales. Also make sure they have curved fingers on each note of the scale.

Here are the notes and the fingering clearly laid out with the moment the 'tunnel' happens written larger than the other numbers:

C - D - E - F - G - A - B - C

1 - 2 - 3 - **1** - 2 - 3 - 4 - 5

TREBLE CLEF: READING LINE NOTES

The next notes for us to learn are the line notes in the treble clef.

E	G	B	D	F
V	O	O	E	U
E	O	Y	S	D
R	D		E	G
Y			R	E
			V	
			E	
			S	

When we memorized the spaces there was a trick, spelling the word F - A - C - E. Learning the line notes, there is also a trick. Teach your child this funny phrase:

| Every | Good | **B**oy | **D**eserves | **F**udge |

The first letter of each word of the phrase is the letter of the note on the staff from top to bottom. This will help them learn their notes faster if they memorize this phrase with it.

Make sure to make individual flashcards for each separate line note in the same format of lesson 1.

SKIPPING NOTES

Up till now, every song we have played the notes have always stepped right next to each other. Notes don't always step. Sometimes they skip. When you see a bigger gap between the notes as well as the fingering skipping over a number that means to skip.

When the fingering skips over a number, the fingers will skip over that finger with fingering which means you are also skipping over that white note. For example if the Right hand has a 1 - 3 - 5 fingering it would mean to start on the 1 'C' note, skip to the 3 'E' note and end on the 5 'G' note.

PRACTICE SONG Lesson 3: To be played by both hands Simultaneously. Top line the right hand bottom line the left hand. Place both hands in C position for the duration of the entire song.

RIGHT

LEFT

Daily Practice Log (4-6 days @ 10-15 minutes each day):

    * Flashcards for terms

    * Flashcards for notes

    * Practice song

    *Corresponding Theory Chapter

    * RH C Scale Going up

(Parent Answer: right hand plays C - D - E - F - G - E - C then the Left hand plays, C - D - E - F - G - E - C....

Repeat last weeks lesson if your child cannot complete its' entire practice log independently.

LESSON 4

C SCALE GOING DOWN RH

To learn going down the C scale, your child must first have a full understanding of going up the C scale. If they have achieved this, then have them play up the scale and hold the C note at the top of the scale.

From that top C note they follow the notes down/backwards until they run out of fingers. C - B - A - G - F using fingers 5 - 4 - 3 - 2 - 1.

I joke with my students, you are out of fingers what happens next? Well, just like we tunneled after the 3 because the 3 finger is so important, we use the same 3 finger to bunny hop over the thumb!

So your child should hold down the thumb on the F note, while the 3 finger bunny hops over and plays the E. As soon as the E plays, then let go of the thumb and shift your hand In line with the 3 thats on the E, so that you can play the rest of the notes. So the notes from the bunny hop on are E - D - C played with 3 - 2 - 1

Here are the notes and the fingering clearly laid out with the moment the 'bunny hop' happens written larger than the other numbers:

C - B - A - G - F - E - D - C
5 - 4 - 3 - 2 - 1 - **3** - 2 - 1

PRACTICE SONG Lesson 4: To be played by both hands Simultaneously. Top line the right hand bottom line the left hand. Place both hands in C position for the duration of the entire song.

RIGHT HAND:

LEFT

Daily Practice Log (4-6 days @ 10-15 minutes each day):
   * *Flashcards for terms*
   * *Flashcards for notes*
   * *Practice song*
   Corresponding Theory Chapter
   * *RH C Scale Going up AND down*

(Parent Answer: right hand plays C - E - G then Left hand, C - E - G, then right hand G - E - C, then left hand G - E - C..... Review with your child skips. This entire song is skips up and skips down.

Repeat last weeks lesson if your child cannot complete its' entire practice log independently.

LESSON 5

READING NOTES ON MUSIC (MIDDLE C)

We have read music using only finger numbers up to this point. Now that you have taught your child the treble clef flashcards, we will begin reading actual notes on the staff. For now we will do a single note, middle C, which means the note itself will be simple, but you still need to pay attention to the rhythms. Have your child count aloud to this weeks practice song as they play it (and all future songs).

STARTING EACH LESSON

I have touched on this subject briefly. I want to make sure you have a detailed plan for teaching your Child's lesson. You should be going over all the new concepts in each lesson. Before doing this however, you should start the lesson with them playing their scales as you check and help them obtain proper technique.

The other start to the lesson should be both terms and notes flashcards.

Before you begin teaching the next weeks lesson, you should hear all their homework from their practice log including the practice song. If any of their homework is challenging for them, that lesson should be repeated instead of moving on.

PRACTICE SONG Lesson 5: The right hand is in C position. *Have your child count aloud to this weeks practice song as they play it (and all future songs). Remember they should be counting 1 - 2 -3 - 4 in each measure*

Daily Practice Log (4-6 days @ 10-15 minutes each day):

  * *Flashcards for terms*

  * *Flashcards for notes*

  * *Practice song*

  Corresponding Theory Chapter

  * *RH C Scale Going up AND down*

Repeat last weeks lesson if your child cannot complete its' entire practice log independently.

parent answer: (all notes played with 1 finger right hand on middle C)

LESSON 6

READING MUSIC WITH NOTES STEPPING UP

Last week you taught your child to read actual music using the note middle C. This week we will learn how to read music when the notes step up.

Notes are stepping up when it alternates between lines and spaces in an upward direction on the page.

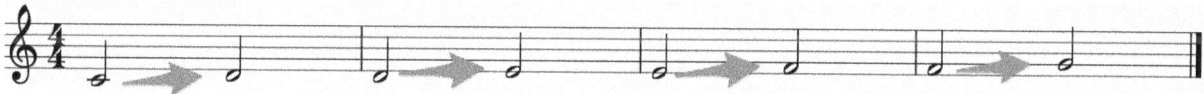

PRACTICE SONG Lesson 6: The right hand is in C position. *To learn a song it is helpful to have them clap and count it aloud before trying to play the notes. Have your child count aloud to this weeks practice song as they play it. Remember they should be counting 1 -2 -3 -4 in each measure.*

Daily Practice Log (4-6 days @ 10-15 minutes each day):
  * Flashcards for terms
  * Flashcards for notes
  * Practice song
  *Corresponding Theory Chapter
  * RH C Scale Going up and down

Repeat last weeks lesson if your child cannot complete its' entire practice log independently.

parent answer:

Note: DO NOT allow your child to see the answer. This is for your reference only that they are completing the practice song correctly.

A child that learns piano by reading the letters written in has not truly learned piano. They will show quick progress initially, but then plateau and never progress beyond a certain point and then tire of piano.

If you find an in person teacher who writes in all or even most of the note names for your child.... RUN!

LESSON 7

READING MUSIC STEPPING UP AND DOWN THE STAFF

You don't have to figure out every note in order to read music. All you have to figure out the first note and then notice the pattern of it going up or down. Going up it will look like its stepping up a mountain, going down it will look like its going down a mountain. Remember stepping notes alternate spaces and line notes.

YOUR CHILD'S TURN TO PLAY:

READING MUSIC WITHOUT ALL THE FINGER NUMBERS WRITTEN IN

When a song is stepping up or down it does not need to write in all the finger numbers. You can see the pattern of the music stepping and that pattern is what tells you to use the next finger number.

PRACTICE SONG Lesson 7: The right hand is in C position. *To learn a song it is helpful to have them clap and count it aloud before trying to learn the notes. Have your child count aloud to this weeks practice song as they play it. Remember they should be counting 1 -2 -3 -4 in each measure*

Daily Practice Log (4-6 days @ 10-15 minutes each day):

> ** Flashcards for terms*
>
> ** Flashcards for notes*
>
> ** Practice song 1 and then 2 once 1 is mastered*
>
> **Corresponding Theory Chapter*
>
> ** RH C Scale Going up and down*

(parent answer C - D - E - E - F - G - G -C)

Repeat last weeks lesson if your child cannot complete its' entire practice log independently.

CHAPTER 4: READING MUSIC ON THE BASS CLEF

LESSON 1

BASS CLEF: READING SPACE NOTES

Starting from the bottom to the top the spaces of the bass clef are A - C - E - G. There is a trick to remember this. With the bass clef spaces teach them the saying **A**ll **C**ows **E**at **G**rass. A trick you can use if they forget this saying is: what animal needs a lot of space? A Cow! So use the cow saying on the LH space.

Make sure to make individual flashcards for each separate space note in the same format of chapter 3 lesson 1.

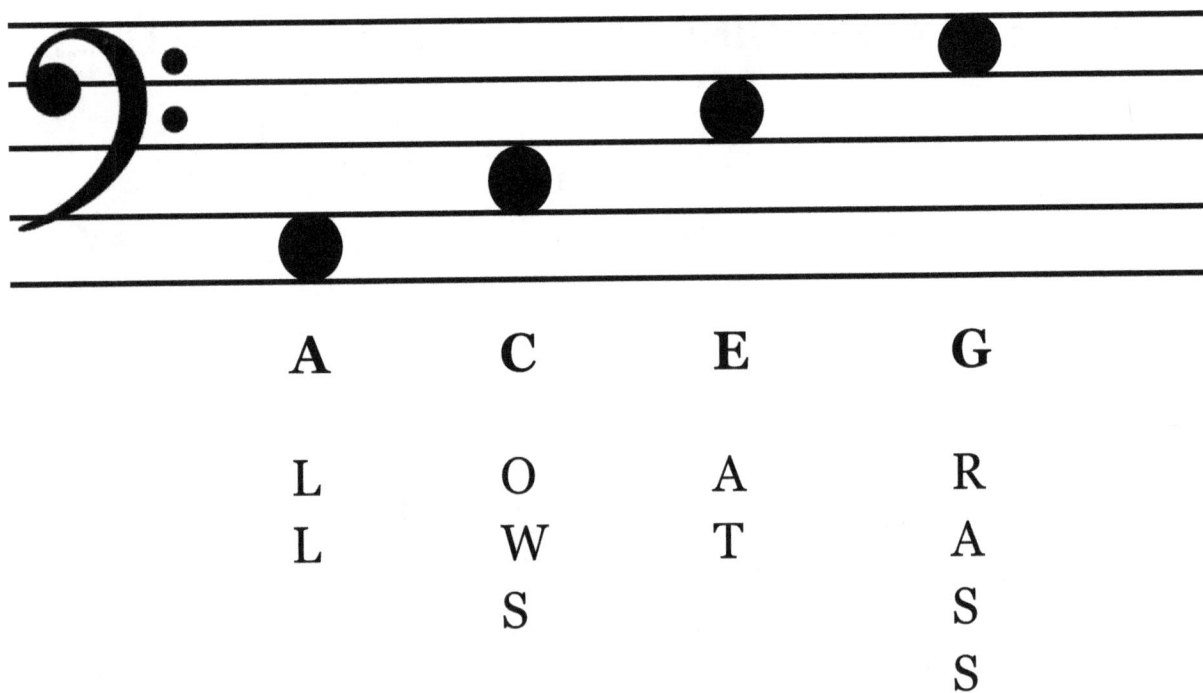

A	C	E	G
L	O	A	R
L	W	T	A
	S		S
			S

STEPPING UP

You have had your child begin to play notes stepping up on the piano in the last couple of lessons. Now, we are going to analyze more specifically how stepping up the staff works so you can help your child recognize steps in their music.

Remind your child of the concept that when the music looks like walking up a mountain it means that you should head up the piano. Refer to the image below.

Now have them look more closely at that image. Point out that the notes alternate from line to space to line to space etc. This is important for them to identify.

It takes both looking like its walking up a mountain as well as alternating line and space notes for it to step up.

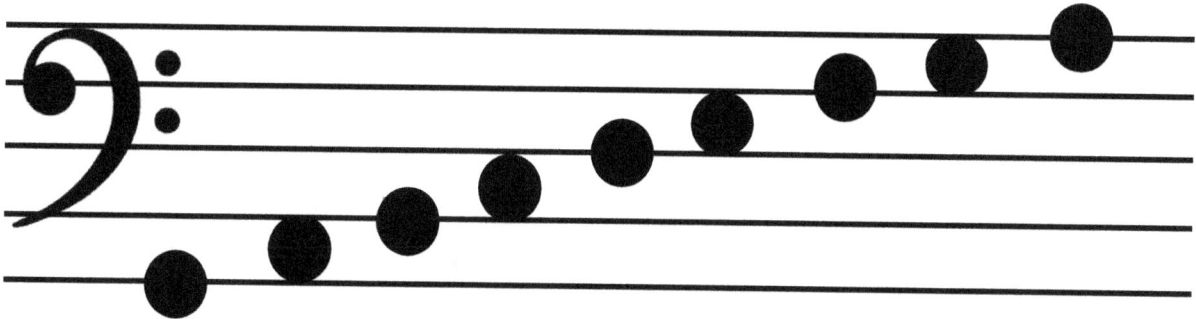

PRACTICE SONG Lesson 1: The LEFT hand is in C position

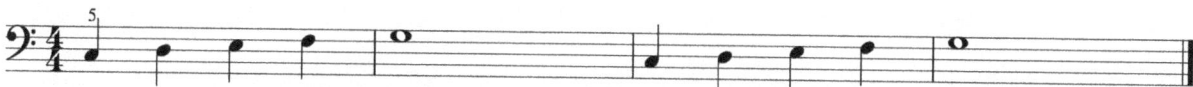

Daily Practice Log (4-6 days @ 10-15 minutes each day):

 * *Flashcards for terms*

  * *Flashcards for treble notes in random order (Do not combine the two clefs flashcards at this point in lessons)*

  **Flashcards for bass notes in random order (Do not combine the two clefs flashcards at this point in lessons)*

 * *Practice song*

 **Corresponding Theory Chapter*

 * *RH C Scale Going up and down*

 **LH C scale going up and down*

Repeat last weeks lesson if your child cannot complete its' entire practice log independently.

(parent answer.. For parent use only):

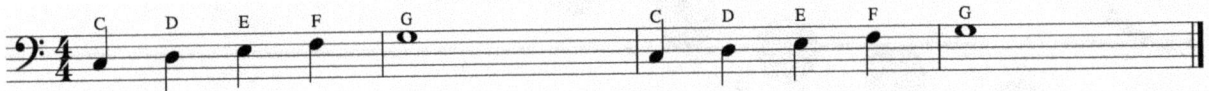

LESSON 2

C SCALE GOING UP LH

Place your child's left hand in C position. They will be playing every single white note from C to C, but with a specific fingering.

It is especially important before beginning that your child has proper hand posture. The hand should be arched (looking like a 'C' shape) with curved fingers.

First, they will play C - D - E - F - G with the fingers 5 - 4 - 3 - 2 - 1. This is the tricky part. As they are holding the 1st finger on G, the 3rd finger will "bunny hop" over to play the next note A.

Once the 3rd finger plays "A" shift the hand so that hand is in line with the 3rd finger. Then play the B and C note with the fingers 2 - 1.

Here are the notes and the fingering clearly laid out with the moment the 'bunny hop' happens written larger than the other numbers:

C - D - E - F - G - A - B - C

5 - 4 - 3 - 2 - 1 - 3 - 2 - 1

Your child's practice days and lessons begins with scales. Have your child do their right hand first and then their left hand once they have completed the right hand

NOTES PLAYED AT THE SAME TIME ON ONE STEM

If you see two note heads connected by the same stem it means that you play them at the exact same time. Point as you explain and read this explanation for your child:

In the example below we see middle C followed by D then those two notes are played simultaneously. In the next measure we see middle C followed by E then those two notes are played simultaneously.

Notice that when multiple notes are played at the same time the note name answer will be written from bottom to top the order they should be played. This will apply to fingering as well as shown in the second example of the same song.

Have your child play the first example with the note names written in and then when they master that have them play the second example with just the finger numbers added.

Sometimes notes are played at the same time that aren't connected by a stem. For example, whole notes do not have a stem. The we know to play them at the same time is when they are located on top of one another as demonstrated in the example to the right.

Played separately

Played Simultaneously

PRACTICE SONG Lesson 2: The LEFT hand is in C position.

Daily Practice Log (4-6 days @ 10-15 minutes each day):

   * Flashcards for terms

    * Flashcards for treble notes in random order (Do not combine the two clefs flashcards at this point in lessons)

    *Flashcards for bass notes in random order (Do not combine the two clefs flashcards at this point in lessons)

   * Practice song

   *Corresponding Theory Chapter

   * RH C Scale Going up and down

   *LH C scale going up and down

Repeat last weeks lesson if your child cannot complete its' entire practice log independently.

(parent answer.. For parent use only):

LESSON 3

<u>BASS CLEF: READING LINE NOTES</u>

Starting from the bottom to the top is a saying to help you remember the bass clef line notes. **G**rizzly **B**ears **D**on't **F**ly **A**irplanes.

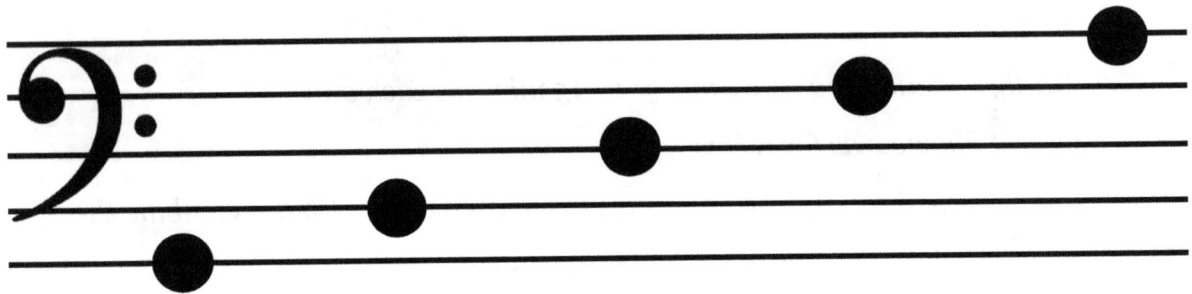

G	**B**	**D**	**F**	**A**
R	E	O	L	I
I	A	N	Y	R
Z	R	T		P
Z	S			L
L				A
Y				N
				E
				S

At this point, many students start confusing all the sayings. A trick to keep them straight is the treble clef sayings have to do with humans (FACE and every good BOY deserves fudge). I tell them the bass clef sayings have to do with animals (all COWS eat grass and grizzly BEARS don't fly airplanes)

Make sure to make individual flashcards for each separate line note in the same format of chapter 3 lesson 1.

STEPPING DOWN

Notes are stepping when it alternates between lines and spaces in an downward direction on the page.

PRACTICE SONG Lesson 3: Both hands are in C position.

Daily Practice Log (4-6 days @ 10-15 minutes each day):

      * Flashcards for terms

        * Flashcards for treble notes in random order (Do not combine the two clefs flashcards at this point in lessons)

        *Flashcards for bass notes in random order (Do not combine the two clefs flashcards at this point in lessons)

      * Practice song

      *Corresponding Theory Chapter

      * RH C Scale Going up and down

      *LH C scale going up

Repeat last weeks lesson if your child cannot complete its' entire practice log independently.

(parent answer... For parent use only):

LESSON 4

C SCALE GOING DOWN LH

To learn going down the C scale, your child must first have a full understanding of going up the C scale in the LH. If they have achieved this, then have them go up the scale and hold the C note at the top of the scale.

From that top C note, they follow the notes down/backwards until the reach the 3rd finger. This is the tricky part. As they're holding the 3rd finger, the thumb will go underneath fingers 2 and 3 to play the next note G with the thumb. I tell the students their hand is a tunnel and the thumb, 1 finger, is going through the tunnel to the next note.

Once they go through the tunnel to play the G note with the 1 finger immediately shift the whole hand so your hand to be in line with the new position of the thumb so it can play the remainder of the notes.

The final notes are F - E - D - C played with fingers 2-3-4-5.

Here are the notes and the fingering clearly laid out with the moment the 'tunnel' happens written larger than the other numbers:

C - B - A - G - F - E - D - C

1 - 2 - 3 - **1** - 2 - 3 - 4 - 5

Note: The fingering is the exact same for the LH and RH but reversed. The RH 'tunnels' under going up and the LH 'tunnels' under going down. The RH 'bunny hops' over going down the LH 'bunny hops' over going up.

NOTES STAYING THE SAME ON THE STAFF

You have taught your child to identify when a note steps up or steps down the staff. Now it is time to teach them recognizing when a note stays the same. If a note stays on the exact same space or line as the previous note, then they should play the same note however many times it is repeated on that spot.

PRACTICE SONG Lesson 4: The LEFT hand is in C position

Daily Practice Log (4-6 days @ 10-15 minutes each day):
* *Flashcards for terms*
   * *Flashcards for treble notes in random order (Do not combing the two clefs flashcards at this point in lessons)*
   * *Flashcards for bass notes in random order (Do not combing the two clefs flashcards at this point in lessons)*
* *Practice song*
Corresponding Theory Chapter
* *C Scale RH then LH going up and down*

Repeat last weeks lesson if your child cannot complete its' entire practice log independently.

(parent answer... for parent use only): The notes are all C. This will be an easier song to learn, so thing to really focus

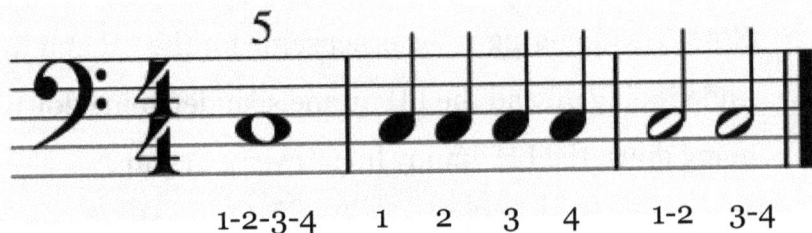

1-2-3-4   1   2   3   4   1-2   3-4

on is the right rhythms, counting aloud with a curved pinky finger.

LESSON 5

NOTES PLAYING THE SAME TIME ON DIFFERENT CLEFS

Review with your child how to recognize when two notes are to be played at the same time because they are connected with one stem.

Teach your child that notes aren't always designated to be played at the same time because a stem connects them. Sometimes we know to play a note in the RH at the same time as a note in the LH because they are lined up perfectly on top of each other. The example below has ALL the notes in the RH playing at the same exact time as the notes in the LH.

Below is an example where the measures alternate between the notes in the two staves being not played together and then played together.

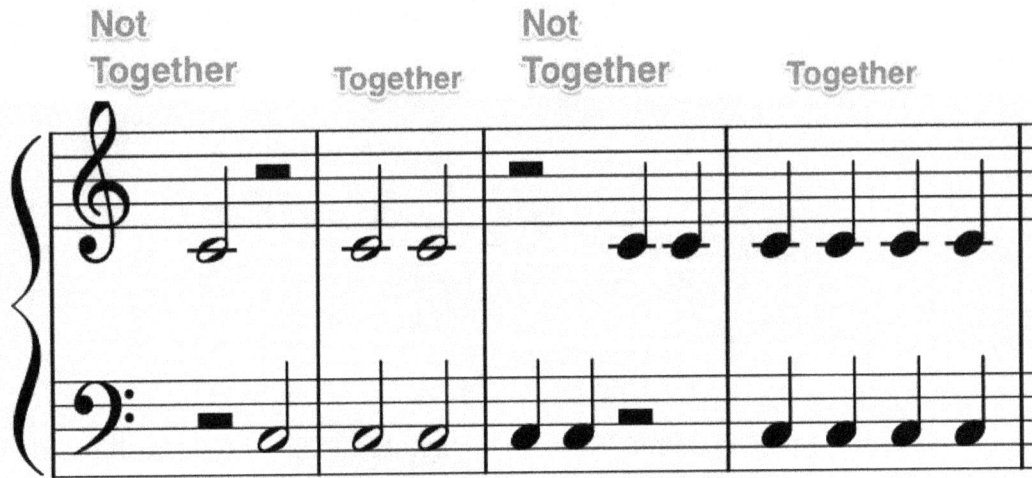

BASS CLEF: READING NOTES MIDDLE C AND B

The next two notes do not have a fun saying. They need to be just memorized. The notes are Middle C and B. Make sure to point out to your child that both of these notes hang above the staff. The C hangs far above the staff with a line through it. It is a line note. The B hangs right above the staff with no line though it making it a space note.

Please make two separate flashcards for the two notes below in the same format that we made the previous flashcards. .

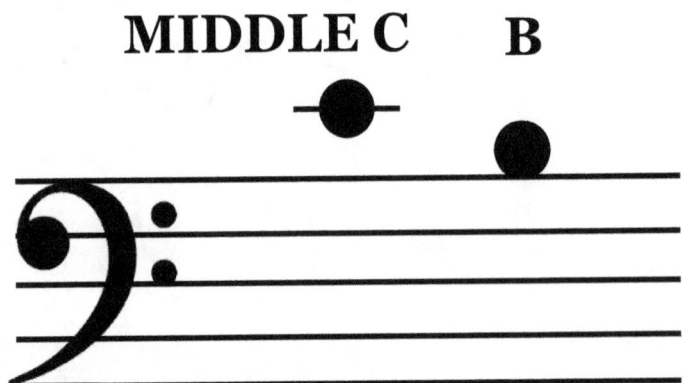

GRAND STAFF

Our next term we will add to the flashcards is Grand Staff. The grand staff is the combination of the treble clef and the bass clef. The grand staff is used to show how to play the right hand and left hand notes at the same time. On the front of the flashcard draw this image and on the back of the flash card write grand staff.

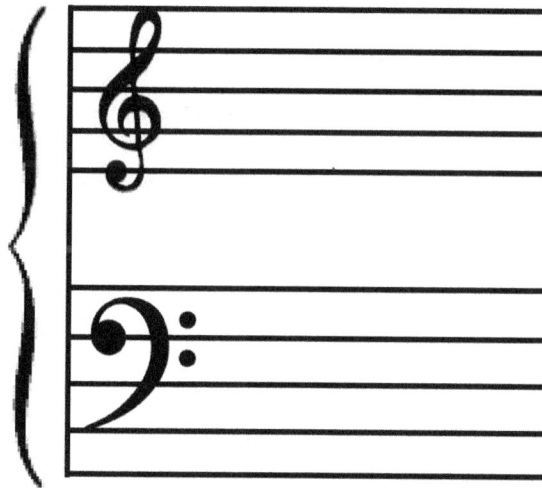

PRACTICE SONG Lesson 5: Both hands are in C position

Daily Practice Log (4-6 days @ 10-15 minutes each day):
* *Flashcards for terms*
  * *Flashcards for treble notes in random order (Do not combine the two clefs flashcards at this point in lessons)*

    Flashcards for bass notes in random order (Do not combine the two clefs flashcards at this point in lessons)
* *Practice song*

  Corresponding Theory Chapter
* *C Scale RH then LH going up and down*

Repeat last weeks lesson if your child cannot complete its' entire practice log independently.

(parent answer... for parent use only):

LESSON 6

HANDS APART SCALE PRACTICE

At this point you child has mastered both the LH and RH C scale going up and down. At every practice session and at every lesson your child should should play first the RH and then the LH scale. If they struggle to complete either hand, then take some time and review how it works and help them remaster that hand's scale.

SLUR

The next term we will add to our flashcards is the term slur. The notes the slur embraces are to be played without separation. (legato). On the front of the flashcard draw the image below and on the back write the slur: musical phrase played legato.

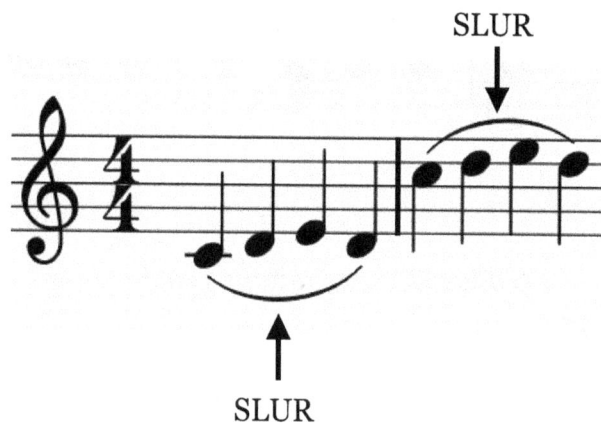

REPEAT

Our next term we will add to the flashcards is repeat. The repeat means to play it again. At this point in lessons, it will always means to go back to the beginning of the song. On the front of the flashcard draw this image and on the back of the flash card write repeat.

PRACTICE SONG Lesson 6: Both hand is in C position

Daily Practice Log (4-6 days @ 10-15 minutes each day):

    * Flashcards for terms

      * Flashcards for treble notes in random order (Do not combine the two clefs flashcards at this point in lessons)

      *Flashcards for bass notes in random order (Do not combine the two clefs flashcards at this point in lessons)

    * Practice song

    *Corresponding Theory Chapter

    * C Scale RH then LH going up and down

Repeat last weeks lesson if your child cannot complete its' entire practice log independently.

(parent answer... for parent use only): The notes are all C's. The thing to focus on is if the notes are directly on top of each other they are played at exactly the same time. Have them Count aloud. Below is the answer of how the counting should occur when two hands play at once. Both hands use the beats at the same time.

CHAPTER 5: SKIPS VERSES STEPS IN MUSIC

LESSON 1

TIME SIGNATURE 4/4

      The next term we will add to the flashcards is the time signature 4/4. A time signature occurs at the beginning of a song. It tells us how many beats to count up to in each measure. So far you have taught your child to count 1-2-3-4 in each measure. This is called a 4/4 (read as four-four) and the symbol you will see associated with it is the image to the right. Anytime you see this symbol at the beginning of the music it means to count 1-2-3-4. On the front of the flashcard draw the image to the right. On the back of the flashcard write 4/4 count to 4.

TIME SIGNATURE 3/4

      The next term we will add to the flashcards is the time signature 3/4. This time signature will be visible at the beginning of the song like all time signatures. It tells us how many beats to count up to in each measure. In this time signature instead of counting 1-2-3-4 in each measure, you now count 1-2-3 in each measure. Anytime you see this symbol at the beginning of the music it means you are in 3/4 (read as three-four) and you count 1-2-3. On the front of the flashcard draw the image to the right. On the back of the flashcard write 3/4 count to 3.

PRACTICE SONG Lesson 1

Daily Practice Log (4-6 days @ 10-15 minutes each day):

*   *Flashcards for terms*
*   *Flashcards for all notes. (Combine the treble and bass clef flashcards*

unless *if your child needs a little more time with them separate.... Make sure the cards*

aren't in order but skip around from each clef and from lines to spaces)

*   *Practice song*

**Corresponding Theory Chapter*

*   *C Scale RH then LH going up and down*

Repeat last weeks lesson if your child cannot complete its' entire practice log

independently.

(parent answer... for parent use only):

LESSON 2

<u>PLAYING AND COUNTING A SONG IN 3/4</u>

You have taught your child to count a 4/4 song. Playing in 3/4 has the exact same principles, the only difference is 3 is the highest number now. Still teach your child to think of the bar line as an eraser line. The bar line erases all the numbers and after the bar line you start over at 1 always.

Practice tip for parents: It is best to write in the counts to a new song. Also, it helps to clap the rhythm counting aloud before beginning to play the notes on the piano.

Here is an example of a rhythm in 3/4 time with the counts underneath. Go over this image with your child, why the counts are the way they are. Then have your child clap the rhythm counting aloud.

Now have your child play the same rhythm above with their RH 1 finger (thumb) on middle C counting aloud.

PRACTICE SONG Lesson 2

Daily Practice Log (4-6 days @ 10-15 minutes each day):

*   * Flashcards for terms*

*   * Flashcards for all notes. (Combine the treble and bass clef flashcards*
unless if your child needs a little more time with them separate.... Make sure the cards
aren't in order but skip around from each clef and from lines to spaces)

*   * Practice song*

*   *Corresponding Theory Chapter*

*   * C Scale RH then LH going up and down*

Repeat last weeks lesson if your child cannot complete its' entire practice log
independently.

(parent answer... for parent use only):

LESSON 3

<u>IDENTIFYING SKIPS IN MUSIC WITH LINES</u>

Up till now your child has only read music going to the very next note either up or down. This was called stepping.

Now we will learn about skipping. There are two ways a note is known to be skipping. The first way is when it goes from one line note to another line note as in this example to the right.

In the above example, we know that the first note is E for the first line of the saying (**E**very good boy deserves fudge). We can easily figure out the next note, not by relying on our flashcard knowledge, but recognizing that it is a line note following a line note. Two lines here mean, if our first note was E, then we must SKIP over the F (space) and play the G note.

In the example below, have your child play and name each of the line notes shown. Before beginning, point out to your child that the notes are climbing UP the mountain, so our skips should head UP the piano as well.

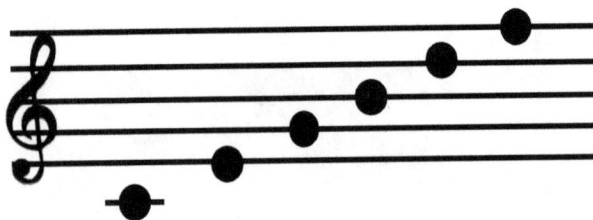

(Parent answer: the whole example was be skips. Your child should have played C-E-G-B-D-F all going up)

Not only do notes skip up the piano, but they can also skip down as well. Recognizing this pattern is especially helpful when going down for young child. It is hard for them to think of the flashcards/notes/alphabet backwards, but recognizing the skipping pattern allows them to not worry about that, for now.

Have your child try this next example playing the skips heading DOWN the piano just like the music looks like it's skipping DOWN the mountain. The first note is an F in the saying (every good boy deserves **F**udge). Have them start on the same F they ended on in the example above.

(Parent answer: the whole example was be skips. Your child should have played F - D - B - G - E - middle C)

IDENTIFYING SKIPS IN MUSIC WITH SPACES

You have taught your child the first way to identify skipping…. by recognizing two line notes next to each other

The second way to recognize a note is skipping is if there are two space notes next to each other like the example to the right.

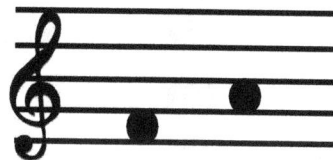

In the previous example, we know that the first note is F for the first letter of the saying **FACE**. We can easily figure out the next note, not by relying on our flashcard knowledge, but recognizing that it is a space note following a space note. Two spaces here means, if our first note was F, then we must SKIP over the G (line) and play the A note.

In the example below, have your child play and name each of the space notes shown. Before beginning, point out to your child that the notes are climbing UP the mountain, so our skips should head UP the piano as well. The only note they have to use their flashcard knowledge for is the very first note.

(Parent answer: the whole example was be skips. Once your child figured out the first note of D, they could skip from there. The notes your child should have played were D - F - A - C - E)

Not only do notes skip up the piano with spaces, but they can also skip down as well. Have your child try this next example playing the skips heading DOWN the piano just like the music looks like its skipping DOWN the mountain. The first note is an E for **FACE**

(Parent answer: the whole example was be skips. Your child should have played E - C - A - F - D).

PRACTICE SONG Lesson 3

Daily Practice Log (4-6 days @ 10-15 minutes each day):

* *Flashcards for terms*

* *Flashcards for all notes. (Combine the treble and bass clef flashcards unless if your child needs a little more time with them separate.... Make sure the cards aren't in order but skip around from each clef and from lines to spaces)*

* *Practice song*

Corresponding Theory Chapter

* *C Scale RH then LH going up and down*

Repeat last weeks lesson if your child cannot complete its' entire practice log independently.

(parent answer... for parent use only):

LESSON 4

IDENTIFYING SKIPS VERSES STEPS IN MUSIC

You have taught your child that steps alternate space and line notes. You have only recently taught them that notes can skip when there are two line notes or two space notes next to one another.

Now, we will teach your child how to alternate between steps and skips in the music. Going from left to right, your child should be looking at each note to determine is the very next note a step or a skip. Go over the image below with your child and then have them play it.

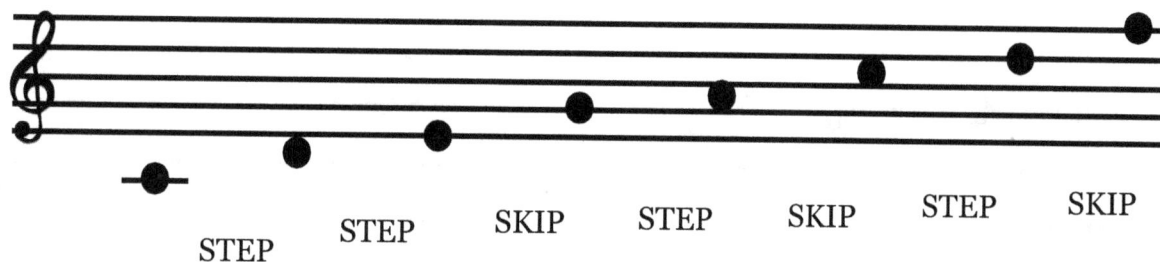

Once your child is able to play the above example and understands the concept, have them play the exact same example again, pictured below, but this time without the step/skip help written in.

Now we are going to teach your child to alternate steps and skips, but this time going down the staff. Going from left to right, your child should be looking at each note to determine if the very next note is a step or a skip. Go over the image below with your child and then have them play it.

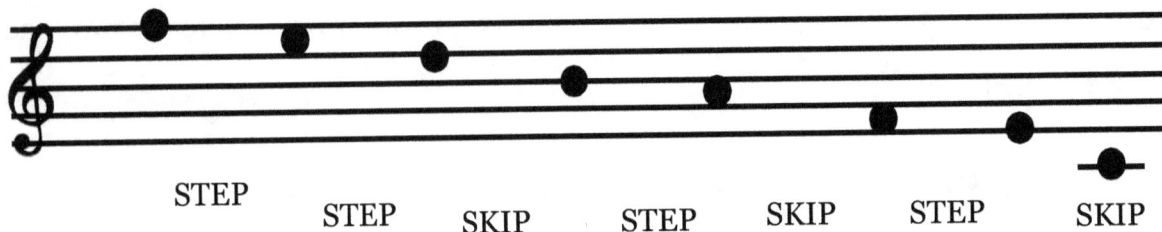

STEP STEP SKIP STEP SKIP STEP SKIP

Once your child is able to play the above example and understands the concept, have them play the exact same example again, pictured below, but this time without the step/skip help written in.

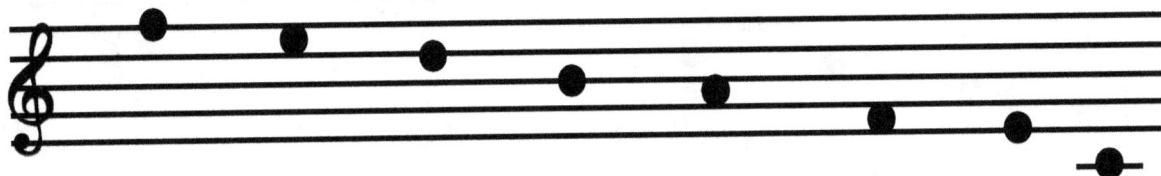

PRACTICE SONG Lesson 4

Daily Practice Log (4-6 days @ 10-15 minutes each day):

    * Flashcards for terms

    * Flashcards for all notes.

    * Practice song

    *Corresponding Theory Chapter

    * C Scale RH then LH going up and down

Repeat last weeks lesson if your child cannot complete its' entire practice log independently.

(parent answer... for parent use only):

LESSON 5

<u>C SCALE GOING UP HANDS TOGETHER</u>

You have taught your child to play the C scale hands apart and they have been playing it successfully for several weeks now. If they still struggle hands apart, really focus on the scale practice so they can master it and move on to this step of playing the C scale in both hands at the same time.

Before beginning remind your child that both of the hands do the exact same thing, but in reverse of each other. So going up the scale the right hand will be tunneling under the 3 finger and the left hand will have the 3rd finger hopping over.

Here is what that will look like:

C - D - E - F - G - A - B - C

RIGHT HAND: 1 - 2 - 3 - 1 - 2 - 3 - 4 - 5

LEFT HAND: 5 - 4 - 3 - 2 - 1 - 3 - 2 - 1

Notice that the "tunnel" and the "bunny hop" do not happen at the exact same time. First comes the tunnel followed two notes later by the bunny hop.

When teaching this to your child take it slow. Have them play just the C's together. Once they do that with ease, then have them play C's to D's together. Once that happens have them do the first 3 notes together.

This is where it'll get harder. While both hands are on the E note have them just hold the note down and really talk through what will happen next. Next the left hand will play the 2 finger on the F, but the right hand will have the thumb tunnel under to the F.

When they master playing the F's together, pause. Make sure they shifted their whole right hand in line with the new thumb position. If everything looks right move on to the G's together which is pretty simple.

Here comes the bunny hop. While holding the G's down in both hands have the LH 3 finger bunny hop over the thumb. Once it's in position to play the A have both hands play the A's together simultaneously. Then, shift the left hand to be in line with the new position of the third finger.

The rest is not too difficult as your Child's hand is in position and ready to play the B's together and then the C's together.

Stop here. Don't try and go down the scale yet. Do this a couple more times throughout the lesson until you're sure you child will be able to practice it during the week.

At this stage, do not have your child go straight to hands together practice each day. Have them play the right hand scale up and down, then the left hand scale up and down. Then have them do hands together going up only.

PRACTICE SONG Lesson 5

Daily Practice Log (4-6 days @ 10-15 minutes each day):

*   * Flashcards for terms*

*   * Flashcards for all notes.*

*   * Practice song*

*   *Corresponding Theory Chapter*

*   * C Scale RH then LH going up and down*

*   *Hands together C scale going up only*

Repeat last weeks lesson if your child cannot complete its' entire practice log independently.

(parent answer... for parent use only):

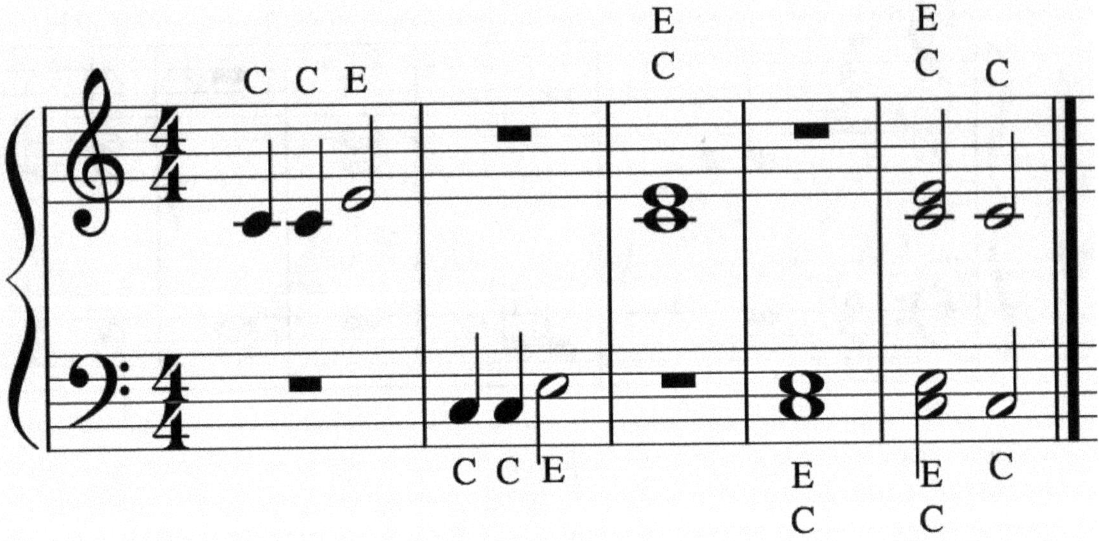

LESSON 6

<u>C SCALE GOING UP AND DOWN HANDS TOGETHER</u>

If your child is able to go up the scale hands together, then move on to teaching them this week about coming back down the scale. If going up the scale hands together is still a big challenge for them, give them another week or two just going up hands together and then at that time return to this part of lesson 6.

Just like when they went up the scale the two hands did the opposite of one another (one tunneled and the other one bunny hopped), the same thing will happen going down except the two hands will switch which one they're doing.

On the way down, the right hand will bunny hop when it runs out of fingers and the left hand will tunnel under after the 3.

The best way to teach going down the scale is to have them go up the scale hands together and stop when they get to the top on that C and rest there. Now you will talk them through each note.

The first two notes are easy cause their fingers are exactly where they should be. So have them go down playing the B's together then the A's together and then have them pause holding down the A's.

On the A, the left hand is on the 3 finger, so it will need to have the 1 finger (thumb) tunnel under to the G. Once its in position, have BOTH hands play the G's at the same time and then shift the left hand to be in position with the new thumb location.

F's together is next and is fairly simple, but it means the right hand has run out of finger. This means the right hand now needs to have the 3rd finger bunny hop over the thumb and get into position to play the E. Once it's in position have the two hands play the E's at the same time. Then have the right hand shift the hand so its in position with the new location of the 3rd finger.

The last two notes are all lined up and ready to go, so have them play the D's then the C's together.

If your child catches on to this concept fairly quickly, they can go straight to hands together C scale in their practice time. If it is a bit of a struggle still, then have their scale practice time be 1)RH hands apart C scale up and down 2) LH hands apart C scale up and down 3)hands together C scale up and down.

PRACTICE SONG Lesson 6

Daily Practice Log (4-6 days @ 10-15 minutes each day):

    * Flashcards for terms

     * Flashcards for all notes. (Combine the treble and bass clef flashcards
    unless if your child needs a little more time with them separate.... Make
    sure the cards aren't in order but skip around from each clef and from
    lines to spaces)

    * Practice song

    *Corresponding Theory Chapter

    * Hands together C Scale going up and down

Repeat last weeks lesson if your child cannot complete its' entire practice log
independently.

(parent answer... for parent use only):

CHAPTER 6: FINDING ON THE PIANO THE NOTES ON THE STAFF

LESSON 1

TIE

The next term to add to our flashcards is the term tie. A tie is a curved line that connects two of the SAME notes. For example two C notes or two D notes. When you see a tie it means those two notes are to be combined and held for the total beats of both notes. On the front of of the flashcard draw the image below and on the back write: tie - means to hold

TIE :

In the example above, F would only play 1 time on the first note. F would hold for 2 beats (2 quarter notes added together equal 2 beats total hold time)

Below is a longer example of how a tie works in a song.
    The first 2 measures the C played once and is held for 8 beats.
    Measure 3 the C is played once and held for 4 beats.
    Measure 4 the C plays, plays again and is held 4 beats going over the bar line

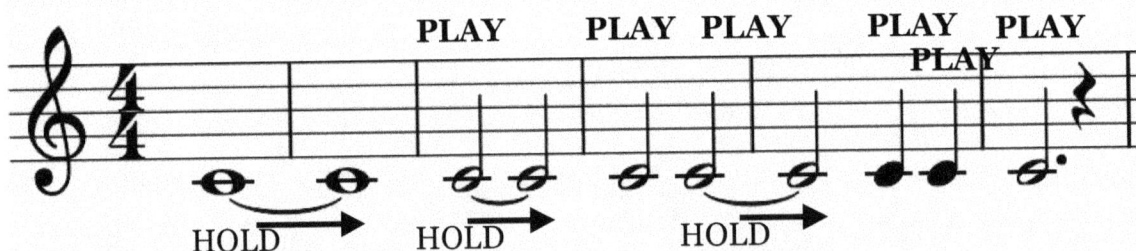

PRACTICE SONG Lesson 1

Daily Practice Log (4-6 days @ 10-15 minutes each day):

* *Flashcards for terms*

* *Flashcards for all notes.*

* *Practice song*

Corresponding Theory Chapter

* *Hands together C Scale going up and down*

Repeat last weeks lesson if your child cannot complete its' entire practice log independently.

(parent answer... for parent use only): (The arrows indicate a tie or a held note)

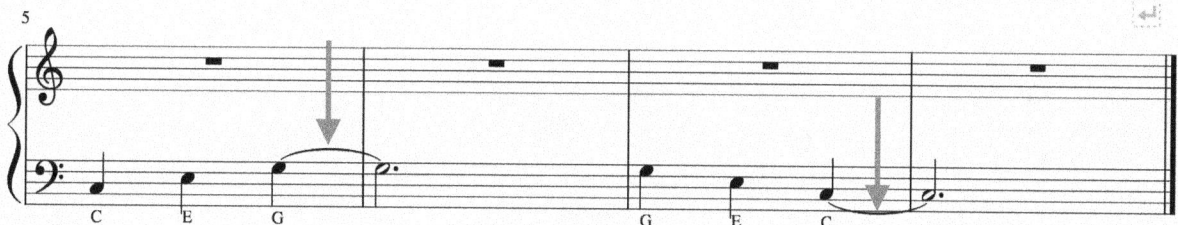

LESSON 2

DIFFERENT C NOTES ON THE PIANO AND STAFF

You have taught your child to identify different notes on their flashcards. Now it is time to teach your kid where those notes are located on the piano more specifically. The C notes are pretty easy because your child already knows C position from their songs.

Middle C is the C right under the words on your piano right in the middle. It is played by your right hand 1 finger in C position

MIDDLE C:

Bass C is the C below middle C. It is played by your left hand 5 finger when your hands are in C position.

BASS C: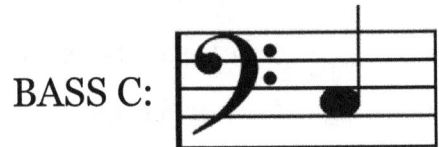

Treble C is the C above middle C. For right now, it is not apart of our songs yet, but it is still important to understand the different locations of the three main C's on the piano.

TREBLE C:

C's on the piano:

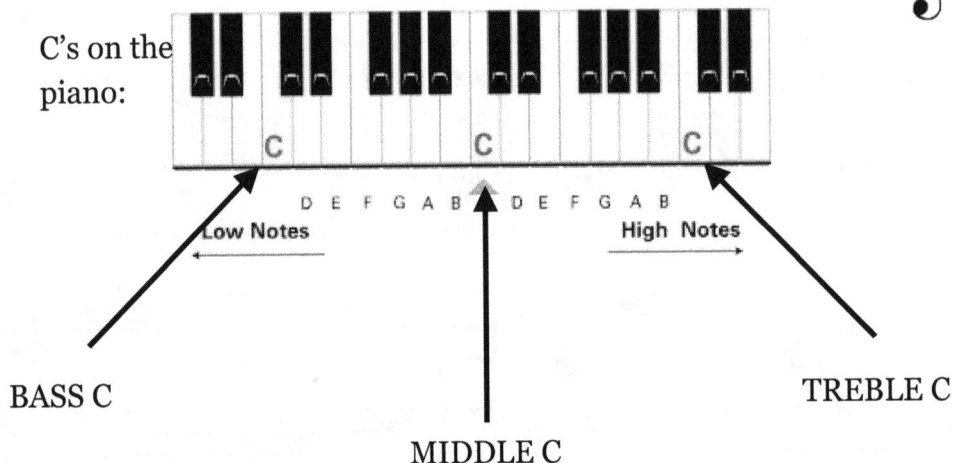

BASS C

MIDDLE C

TREBLE C

YOUR CHILD'S TURN TO PLAY:

Take out the 3 C's that they have learned in their flashcards (treble, middle and bass). Mix up those 3 flashcards and as you hold up each card have your child find the correct C location on the piano to match the flashcard. Do this until your child has a good grasp on the concept.

PRACTICE SONG Lesson 2

Daily Practice Log (4-6 days @ 10-15 minutes each day):

   * *Flashcards for terms*

   * *Flashcards for all notes.*

   * *Practice song*

   Corresponding Theory Chapter

   * *Hands together C Scale going up and down*

   Identify bass, middle, treble C

Repeat last weeks lesson if your child cannot complete its' entire practice log independently.

(parent answer... for parent use only): The arrow indicates a tie or held note.)

LESSON 3

<u>SLUR</u>

The next term to add to the flashcards is Slur. A slur is similar in appearance to a tie. A slur is a musical phrase and it means the notes inside of it need to be played legato. On the front of the flashcard draw the image below and on the back write: slur - musical phrase played legato.

<u>SLUR VERSUS A TIE</u>

Although they both look similar, a slur is joining notes that are DIFFERENT from each other and a tie is joining notes that are the SAME as each other.

Tie   Slur

<u>DIFFERENT D NOTES ON THE PIANO AND STAFF</u>

Just like the different C's on the piano are designated by their location on the staff (the flashcards) the same principle applies to all the other notes as well. Let's teach your child how to also identify the different D's on the piano.

Middle D is the D right next to middle C. It is played by your right hand 2 finger in C position

MIDDLE D:

Bass D is the D below middle D. It is played by your left hand 4 finger when your hands are in C position.

BASS D:

Treble D is the D above middle D. For right now, it is not apart of our songs, but it is still important to understand the different locations of the three main D's on the piano.

TREBLE D:

D's on the piano:

D E F G A B   D E F G A B
Low Notes   High Notes

BASS D

MIDDLE D

TREBLE D

YOUR CHILD'S TURN TO PLAY:

Take out the 3 D's that they have learned in their flashcards (treble, middle and bass). Mix up those 3 flashcards and as you hold up each card have your child find the correct D location on the piano to match the flashcard. Do this until your child has a good grasp on the concept.

Then Add the 3 C flashcards and mix up the C and D flashcards and see if your child can identify both C's and D's in the correct spot on the piano.

PRACTICE SONG Lesson 3

Daily Practice Log (4-6 days @ 10-15 minutes each day):
  * *Flashcards for terms*
   * *Flashcards for all notes.*
  * *Practice song*
  Corresponding Theory Chapter
  * *Hands together C Scale going up and down*
  Identify bass, middle, treble C and D

Repeat last weeks lesson if your child cannot complete its' entire practice log independently.

(parent answer... for parent use only): (The arrow indicates a tie or held note. The star indicates a slur or musical phrase played legato)

LESSON 4

<u>LEGATO</u>

Legato is the next term to add to our flashcards. It is a term that means the the notes are played smooth and connected without a break in sound between each note. On the front of the flashcard write Legato. On the back write smooth and connected.

<u>DIFFERENT E NOTES ON THE PIANO AND STAFF</u>

You have taught your child to identify the different C's and D's on the piano. Let's end this chapter with learning the different E's on a piano

Middle E is the E 2 notes above middle C. It is played by your right hand 3 finger in C position

MIDDLE E:

Bass E is the E below middle E. It is played by your left hand 3 finger when your hands are in C position.

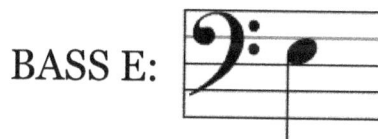

BASS E:

Treble E is the E above middle E. For right now, it is not apart of our songs, but it is still important to understand the different locations of the three main E's on the piano.

TREBLE E:

E's on the piano:

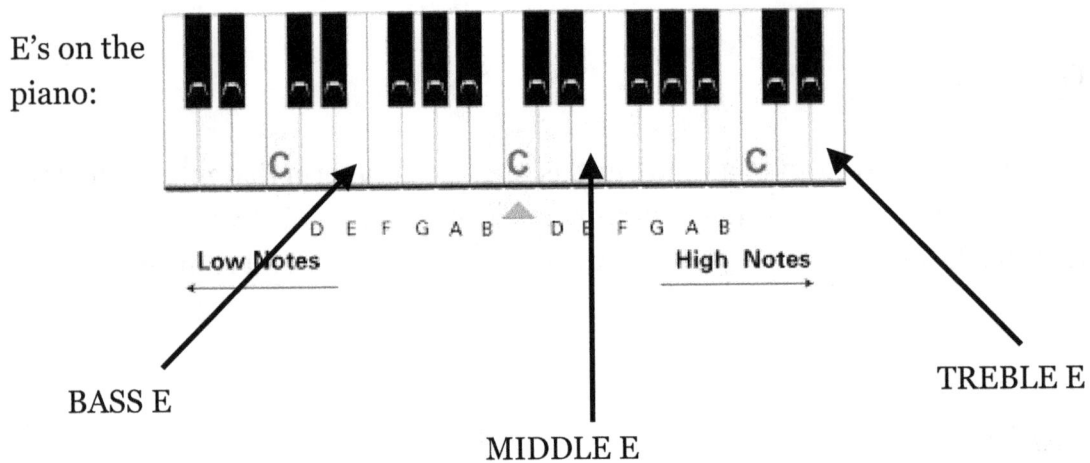

BASS E

MIDDLE E

TREBLE E

YOUR CHILD'S TURN TO PLAY:

Take out the 3 E's that they have learned in their flashcards (treble, middle and bass). Mix up those 3 flashcards and as you hold up each card have your child find the correct E location on the piano to match the flashcard. Do this until your child has a good grasp on the concept.

Then Add the 3 C & D flashcards and combine the C and D flashcards with the E flashcards and see if your child can identify C's, D's & E's in the correct spot on the piano.

PRACTICE SONG Lesson 4

Daily Practice Log (4-6 days @ 10-15 minutes each day):

> ** Flashcards for terms*
>
> ** Flashcards for all notes.*
>
> ** Practice song*
>
> **Corresponding Theory Chapter*
>
> ** Hands together C Scale going up and down*
>
> **Identify bass, middle, treble C and D, E*

Repeat last weeks lesson if your child cannot complete its' entire practice log independently.

(parent answer... for parent use only): (The arrow indicates a tie or held note. The star indicates a slur or musical phrase played legato) notice: the left hand is tied for the entire piece. It plays the first note and then holds down the rest of the time never letting go of the initial notes.

CHAPTER 7: THE QUARTER REST

LESSON 1

QUARTER REST

The next term to add to your flashcards is the quarter rest. The quarter rest is equal in value to the quarter note. The only difference instead of getting 1 beat of the note playing, you get 1 beat of silence. So for 1 beat, nothing is played on the piano. On the front of the flashcard draw the image below and on the back write quarter rest - 1 beat of silence.

PLAYING LEGATO

You have already taught your child that legato means to play smooth and connected. Now it is time to make sure they are applying that principle to their playing.

Specifically make sure their daily scale practice is done legato. The best way to do that is have them play the C's. Don't let go of the C's until the moment the D's play. Then don't let go of the D's until the exact moment the E's play. Very slowly talk them through the same process for each note.

Their scale might get slower for a while until the legato concept comes easier to them. That's alright. It's more important that they are playing their scales with curved fingers and legato than they play it fast.

As they master the legato concept, have them apply it to any songs they are learning. Specifically, make sure they are playing all their slurs legato (holding on to the note played and not letting go until the exact moment the next note plays).

PRACTICE SONG Lesson 1 - song is in C position

Daily Practice Log (4-6 days @ 10-15 minutes each day):

* *Flashcards for terms*

* *Flashcards for all notes.*

* *Practice song*

Corresponding Theory Chapter

* *Hands together C Scale going up and down*

Identify bass, middle, treble C and D, E

Repeat last weeks lesson if your child cannot complete its' entire practice log independently.

(parent answer... for parent use only): notice the repeat at the end of the song. This means your child upon reaching the repeat starts the whole thing over again to play it a total of 2 times.

LESSON 2

BINGO SONG ILLUSTRATES QUARTER REST

The song Bingo is a great example to use with your child to illustrate the quarter rest. The song, the first time, sings straight through like normal: "There was a farmer who had a dog and bingo was his name - o. B-I-N-G-O, B-I-N-G-O, B-I-N-G-O and bingo was his name-o."

The next time through the song, when it spells out the name Bingo, the B is replaced with a hand clap and then only I-N-G-O is sung. That hand clap on the letter B is the equivalent to 1 quarter rest. As they sing this and clap hold up the quarter rest flash card at the same time as the clap.

Do this for the entire Bingo song as your child sings and claps.

Now explain to your child that with a quarter rest in music we don't clap it, we have silence. At this level, it's best if your child says "shhh" each time there is a quarter rest.

Now, that you explained a quarter rest gets a "shhh" and not a clap, redo the Bingo song. This time as you hold up the quarter rest flashcard have your child say "shh" for each missing letter and not clap to demonstrate how the rest will work in their songs.

For example, the third time throughout the song as they are saying "shh" for the missing letters it will sound like this: "There was a farmer who had a dog and bingo was his name-o. SHH-SHH-N-G-O, SHH-SHH-N-G-O, SHH-SHH-N-G-O, and bingo was his name-o.

CLAPPING THE QUARTER REST RHYTHM

Now you will need to teach your child how to apply the same "shh" for the quarter rest into their actual songs. Your child's songs are getting harder, so at this point, before they play the song, they should clap and count the song out loud.

YOUR CHILD'S TURN TO PLAY:

Have your child clap this song and count aloud. Don't have them play it yet.

Parent answer: (notice how the "shh" replaced the number it took the place of. Also, notice the half note in the last measure. That clap will hold in place for two beats, let go on beat 3 for the rest and then clap again on beat 4)

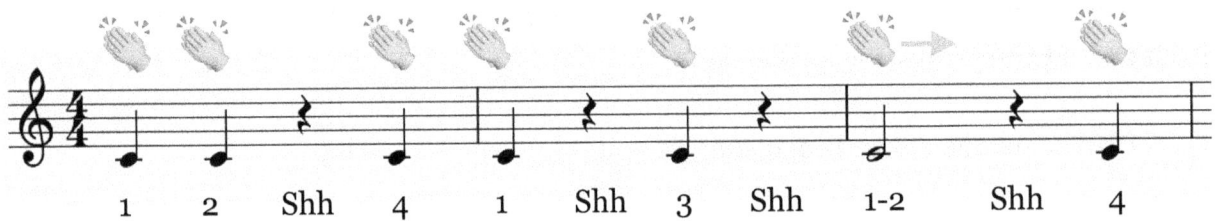

1   2   Shh   4   1   Shh   3   Shh   1-2   Shh   4

Alternate Parent answer: If your child is older, they may be able to say the number instead of saying shh and just remain silent for that number. If your child is able to do that, they would count like the answer below and during the number with a rest above it remain silent on the piano as they say the number.

1   2   3   4   1   2   3   4   1-2   3   4

PRACTICE HABITS

This is the practice method that should be used on all songs from here on out.

1st clap the whole song counting aloud.
2nd practice playing just the right hand counting aloud.
3rd practice playing just the left hand counting aloud.
4th when all that can be done with ease put the hands together playing at the same time counting aloud.

PRACTICE SONG Lesson 2 - song is in C position

(note: this song is the same exact rhythm as the practice exercises in the lesson).

Daily Practice Log (4-6 days @ 10-15 minutes each day):
   * Flashcards for terms
      * Flashcards for all notes.
   * Practice song
   *Corresponding Theory Chapter
   * Hands together C Scale going up and down
   *Identify bass, middle, treble C and D, E

Repeat last weeks lesson if your child cannot complete its' entire practice log independently.

(parent answer... for parent use only): note: This is the same rhythm as our examples in the lesson

Lesson 3

PLAYING MUSIC WITH QUARTER RESTS

Before playing any piece, have your child clap and count it aloud. This will help them to not be overwhelmed playing the correct notes and the correct rhythm. They will have already mastered the rhythms before attempting the notes

What to teach and show your child in the music is that even though the notes are not right next to each other because they are separated by the rests, it is important to look from the first note to the very next note to see if they are stepping or skipping. For this lesson we will have all the notes step and not skip.

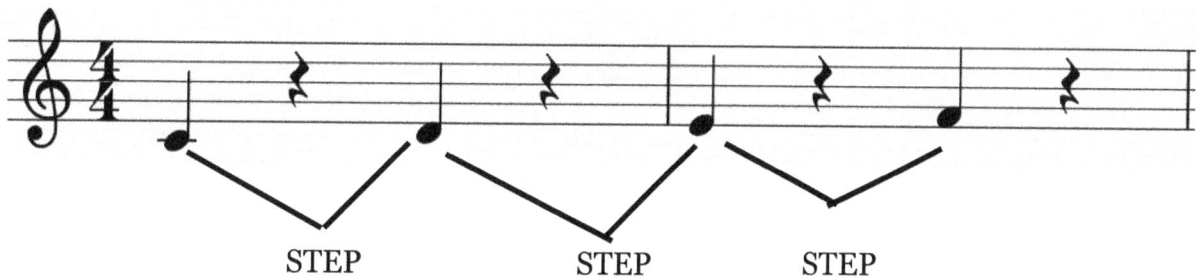

Notice in the example above that even though you counted the rest, you had to look beyond the rest to the next note to see that you were stepping from C to D to E to F.

YOUR CHILD'S TURN TO PLAY:

Have your child clap this song and count aloud. Then have them play the song while counting on the piano.

Parent answer to lesson example:

PRACTICE SONG Lesson 3 - song is in C position

(note: this song is the same exact rhythm as the practice exercises in the lesson).

Daily Practice Log (4-6 days @ 10-15 minutes each day):
    * Flashcards for terms
     * Flashcards for all notes.
    * Practice song
    *Corresponding Theory Chapter
    * Hands together C Scale going up and down
    *Identify bass, middle, treble C and D

Repeat last weeks lesson if your child cannot complete its' entire practice log independently.

(parent answer... for parent use only):

Lesson 4

READING MUSIC WITH SKIPS AND QUARTER RESTS

Just like reading music with steps and quarter rests, the same principles apply to skips. Even though you have to count and be quiet during the rest, you must look beyond the rest to the next note to determine if the note is skipping or stepping.

Review with your child, that a note is skipping when it goes from one line note to another note or one space note to another space note. It is stepping if it is alternating lines and space notes.

Notice on the example above, there are several things that happen. Notes stay the same, skip and step. Each one is separated by a beat of silence, so you need to show your child to look for the pattern from note to note ignoring the rests even though you are giving them their due silence. In the example above it went C - E - E - F - F - A with a beat of silence between each note.

YOUR CHILD'S TURN TO PLAY:

After using the example above as a teaching aid, have your child clap the same example with the answers removed and count aloud. Then have them play the song while counting on the piano.

PRACTICE SONG Lesson 4 - song is in C position

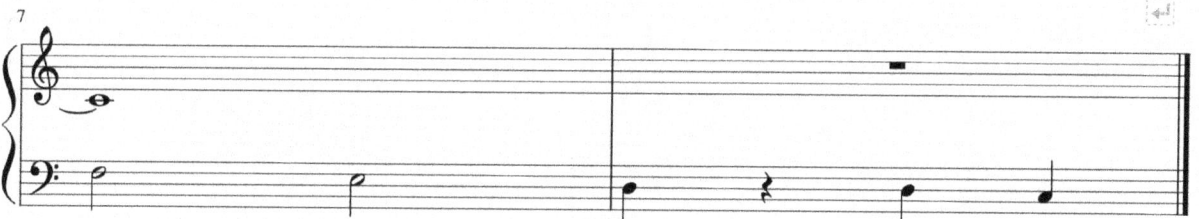

Daily Practice Log (4-6 days @ 10-15 minutes each day):
  * Flashcards for terms
    * Flashcards for all notes.
  * Practice song
  *Corresponding Theory Chapter
  * Hands together C Scale going up and down
  *Identify bass, middle, treble C and D, E

Repeat last weeks lesson if your child cannot complete its' entire practice log independently.

(parent answer... for parent use only):

Lesson 5

READING MUSIC WITH QUARTER RESTS AND TIES

    You have taught your child to identify steps and skips while playing quarter rests. Now you will teach them how to count and play ties within a song that has quarter rests.

    This can be a challenging concept at first because to a child a rest and a tie can sound and feel the same. But they are different. A tie is holding the note down so the sound carries longer. A rest is completely removing the fingers from playing any note on the piano having complete silence.

    In the example below, show your child where you hold the note verses where there is a "shh." Every example and song should start with clapping the rhythm aloud first. Remember a tie you hold your 1 clap (for 2 notes) in place for the duration of those 2 notes)

Notice in the example above there are steps and skips in the music that your child will need to watch out for.

YOUR CHILD'S TURN TO PLAY:

    After using the example above as a teaching aid, have your child clap the same example with the answers removed and count aloud. Then have them play the song while counting on the piano.

PRACTICE SONG Lesson 5 - song is in C position

(note: this song is the same exact rhythm as the practice exercises in the lesson).

Daily Practice Log (4-6 days @ 10-15 minutes each day):

   * *Flashcards for terms*

      * *Flashcards for all notes.*

   * *Practice song*

   Corresponding Theory Chapter

   * *Hands together C Scale going up and down*

   Identify bass, middle, treble C and D, E

Repeat last weeks lesson if your child cannot complete its' entire practice log independently.

(parent answer... for parent use only): Note: the whole notes are tied as well, but that should be easier to identify without a written aid. The only "tie" answers are for the more complicated ones at this point in the book.

CHAPTER 8: STACCATOS AND ACCIDENTALS

Lesson 1

<u>SHARP</u>

The next term that we will add to our flashcards is the term sharp. A sharp has a very technical definition that we will simplify for now. Teach your child that when they see the sharp symbol it means to go UP to the black note above the note shown. On the front of the flashcard draw the symbol to the right. On the back of the flashcards write Sharp - go UP to the next black note

There is a little trick I use to help kids remember that a sharp means to go up. Sharp sounds like shark and a shark comes up out of the water to take a bite of you. Then I tickle my kids as I say that. The physical memory of laughing while talking about sharps reminds them of sharks which reminds them to go up.

In this book, we will not be playing sharps in our song. We will be learning about sharps and practicing them in our theory so that your child has a strong understanding of sharps before moving on to the next book where they will learn to play them in their songs.

Below are two examples that show how sharps look on the staff, in your music. Then next to that is an example of how that sharp in music would be played on the piano.

Ex. 1:

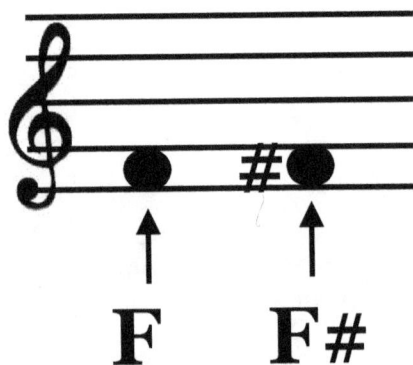

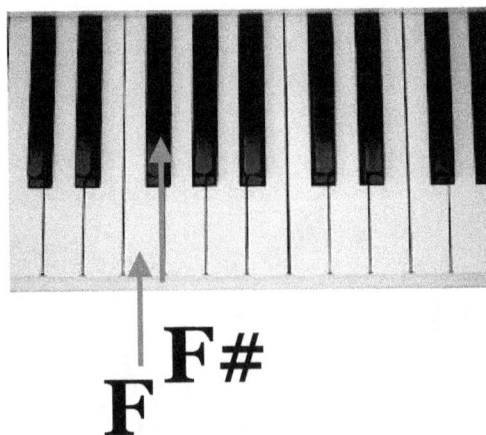

Ex. 2

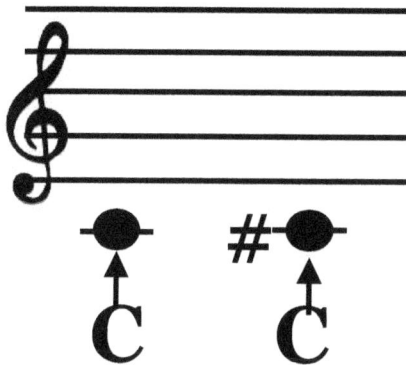

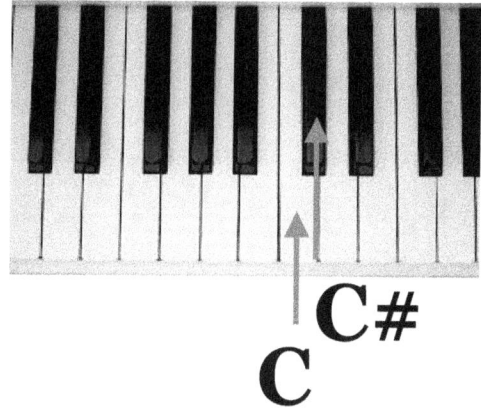

YOUR CHILD'S TURN TO PLAY:

Now that you have explained the concept of reading sharps and finding those notes on the piano to your child, have your child do the same examples, but without the answers written in. Have them say allowed the names of the notes on the staff and then have them play those notes on the piano. The first two examples are the same as the ones above. Example 3 is a new example without an answer above.

EX. 1

EX. 3

EX. 2

PRACTICE SONG Lesson 1 - song is in C position

Daily Practice Log (4-6 days @ 10-15 minutes each day):
  * Flashcards for terms
  * Flashcards for all notes.
  * Practice song
  *Corresponding Theory Chapter
  * Hands together C Scale going up and down
  *Identify bass, middle, treble C and D, E

Repeat last weeks lesson if your child cannot complete its' entire practice log independently.

(parent answer... for parent use only): Note: the whole notes are tied as well, but that should be easier to identify without a written aid. The only "tie" answers are for the more complicated ones at this point in the book.

Lesson 2

FLAT

The next term that we will add to our flashcards is the term flat. A flat has a very technical definition that we will simplify for now. Teach your child that when they see the flat symbol it means to go DOWN to the black note below the note shown. On the front of the flashcard draw the symbol to the right. On the back of the flashcards write flat - go DOWN to black note below

There is a little trick I use to help kids remember that a flat means to go down. Have your child lay flat on the ground. Then I ask them when you're flat on the ground like that are you up or down? The physical memory of laying down while talking about flats reminds them flats need to go down. If they forget down the road, they don't need to lay on the ground every time. Just remind them "when you're flat on the ground which direction are you up or down? When they answer down remind them flats go down.

In this book, we will not be playing flats in our songs. We will be learning about flats and practicing them in our theory so that your child has a strong understanding of flats before moving on to the next book where they will learn to play them in their songs.

Below are two examples that show how flats look on the staff, in your music. Then next to that is an example of how that flat in music would be played on the piano.

Ex. 1:

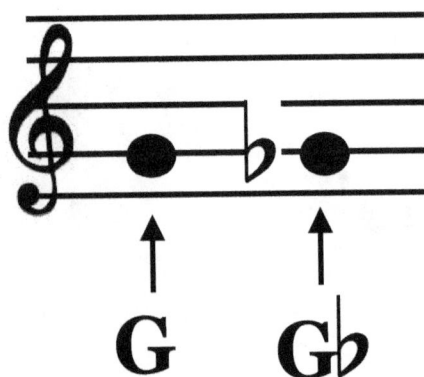

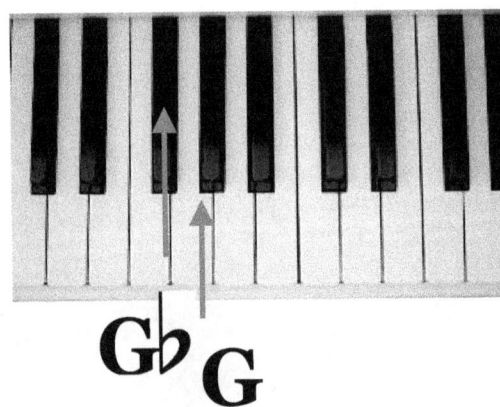

Ex. 2

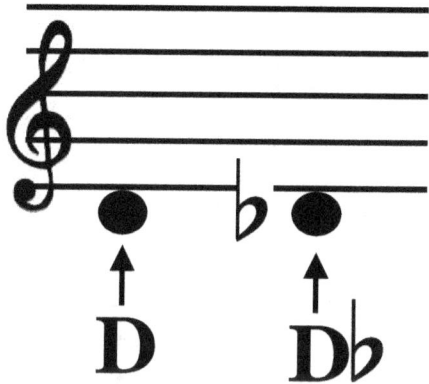

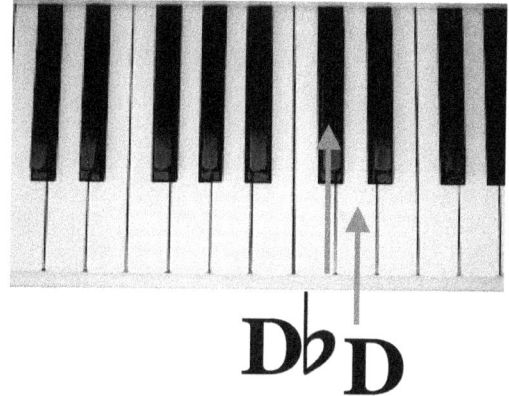

YOUR CHILD'S TURN TO PLAY:

Now that you have explained the concept of reading flats and finding those notes on the piano to your child, have your child do the same examples, but without the answers written in. Have them say aloud the names of the notes on the staff and then have them play those notes on the piano. The first two examples are the same as the ones above. Example 3 is a new example without an answer above.

EX. 1

EX. 3

EX. 2

PRACTICE SONG Lesson 2

Practice habits: Reminder that you should still be utilizing the practice habits outlined in Chapter 7 lesson 2 before every practice song.

Daily Practice Log (4-6 days @ 10-15 minutes each day):
- *Flashcards for terms*
- *Flashcards for all notes.*
- *Practice song*
- *Corresponding Theory Chapter*
- *Hands together C Scale going up and down*
- *Identify bass, middle, treble C and D, E*

Repeat last weeks lesson if your child cannot complete its' entire practice log independently.

(parent answer... for parent use only):

Lesson 3

<u>Staccato</u>

    The next term we will add to our flashcard is staccato. Staccato means a note that is sharply detached or separated from the other notes. On the front of your flashcard draw the image to the right and on the back write staccato: to play short/detached.

    A staccato means to play the note short. It is played almost like the note is a hot potato and they have to jump off the note. It is the opposite of playing legato. A common mistake with staccatos are because it means to play the note short children often play them in very fast succession. It is important to teach your child that their counting should not get faster but stay slow and steady. Just as they "hop" off the note they will wait in the air for the next beat when they will play.

    Notice in the image to the right that the dot can happen either above or below the note to show a staccato. A lot of children confuse the staccato with a dotted half note because the dotted half note also has a dot. Notice that the dotted half note has the dot on the SIDE of the note NOT above or below it. That is how you can tell the difference between the two.

<u>Ex. 1</u> - Slurs and staccato stepping up

Ex. 2 - skips with rests. First with no staccato and then with staccato.

PRACTICE SONG Lesson 3 - song is in C position

Daily Practice Log (4-6 days @ 10-15 minutes each day):
  * Flashcards for terms
    * Flashcards for all notes.
  * Practice song
  *Corresponding Theory Chapter
  * Hands together C Scale going up and down
  *Identify bass, middle, treble C and D, E

Repeat last weeks lesson if your child cannot complete its' entire practice log independently.

(parent answer... for parent use only): Make sure your child's slur's are played legato. Notice the staccato's starting in measure 7. Make sure your child does not speed up their counting as they "hop" off the staccato notes. Notice that many of the rhythms and notes in the practice song are the same as from the lesson.

Lesson 4

<u>PREPARING FOR A RECITAL</u>

This book should take 6-12 months to complete... basically one school year. At the end of each school year teachers typically have a piano recital. This is a great motivator for students to stay excited about learning piano.

At a recital, they can tangibly see the fruits of their labor. They see that they worked really hard and then they were able to create something really beautiful and they were celebrated for their hard work by the friends and family that come to the recital.

It is possible to create that memorable experience for your child while they are in this book. This lesson we will be learning their final homework song. This song will be the hardest one they have learned yet because it will have most of the elements we have learned as well as it will be a little longer.

Take several weeks to master this lesson's song. Get the song to the point where it is almost easy for your child to play well. Even if it takes 3-4 weeks that is ok. It is normal to take longer on a song that will be performed for a recital. Use the time mastering this song to solidify all the skills of this level.

Once this song is mastered, schedule an online recital for your child. Use zoom or facebook live or some other live platform for those that can't attend and have those that can attend sitting on the couches as their audience. Have your child dress up and have them stand in front of the piano, say their name and the name of their song. Then have them sit at the piano and play their piece. When they are done have them bow to the audience/camera and everyone applaud. Then have a little celebration for them with cookies and lemonade or whatever their favorite treats are.

This will give them the motivation to continue learning piano as well as give them the special memories they will cherish their whole life. These memories were made with YOU being their teacher. That is a priceless gift.

<u>MOVING ON TO THE NEXT LEVEL</u>

This is the last lesson of this book before moving on to the next level. Your child deserves a lot praise, that's quite an accomplishment!

Before starting the next book, it is very important that every concept taught in this book is understood by your child. If there is something your child still struggles with, take a few weeks and focus on that skill to help your child master it. Piano is like math. The skills build upon one another and if you move on without a strong foundation your child will quickly become frustrated and loose interest in the piano.

Finishing this book is the equivalent of finishing any of the first lesson books in-person teachers typically use. In the Faber piano adventure series and the Bastien piano basic method book your child has done the equivalent of finishing their primer level book and your child should be ready to begin their level 1. I personally prefer the Faber series, but either are a good method book.

If you would like to wait a little longer before finding an in person teacher, your child is still at a beginning enough level that the parent is perfectly capable of teaching them and moving on to the next level of this book. Just make sure that they are having curved fingers on every note and their wrist is level with their hand not higher or lower than their hand. Those are the two biggest technique elements that an in-person teacher would help correct at this stage.

Moving on to the next level of this book would be the equivalent of moving on to the second book (level 1) of Bastien or Faber series. Each book in this series typically take 6 months to a year to complete on average so you be saving up to another years worth of lessons.

There is not just a monetary advantage to continuing with this book to the next level. There is a direct correlation in piano students success with how involved the parents are. Parents that sit in on the lesson and sit in on their child's practice time to make sure they are practicing correctly have children who are far more successful at the piano and learn at a faster rate.

You learning alongside your child in these first few levels is giving you an understanding of piano so that you can continue to help them as they move on to more advanced levels.

RECITAL SONG Lesson 4 - song is in C position

Practice habits: 1st clap the whole song counting aloud. 2nd practice playing just the right hand counting aloud. 3rd practice playing just the left hand counting aloud. 4th when all that can be done with ease put the hands together playing at the same time counting aloud. This is the practice method that should be used on all songs from here on out. (note: this song is the same exact rhythm as the practice exercises in the lesson).

    note: the practice habits are even more important now as the songs increase in difficulty. It is common to take one week and do nothing but hands apart practice. At the lesson the following week if the student mastered it hands apart, then and only then begin learning it hands together. Help them with hands together to understand how the two hands go back and forth and play at the same time.

Daily Practice Log (4-6 days @ 10-15 minutes each day):
*   * Flashcards for terms
     * Flashcards for all notes.
*   * Practice song
*   *Corresponding Theory Chapter
*   * Hands together C Scale going up and down
*   *Identify bass, middle, treble C and D, E

Repeat last weeks lesson if your child cannot complete its' entire practice log independently.

(parent answer... for parent use only):

Other Resources From This Author:

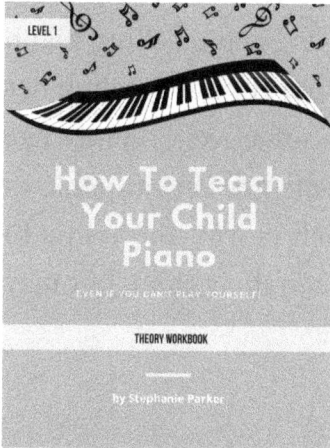

How To Teach Your Child Piano
Level 1 Theory Workbook

This theory workbook is meant to be a supplement to the corresponding teaching book. Unlike the teaching book, which needs direct parent involvement, this theory book may function more independently.

Buy today on amazon.com

Join the Parker Music Academy
Online Community

Free resources, Online Course, Community of like-minded parents and teachers and more.

parkermusicacademy.us

About the Author:

Stephanie Parker has played classical piano for over 35 years. She attended Florida State University College of Music with a concentration in piano. She has been teaching piano for over 20 years as well as been a homeschooling mom since 2006. Homeschooling her children has given her a unique skill set to learn how to teach effectively mainly age ranges with many differing abilities. It has also shown her parents are very capable of teaching their children many subjects with the proper help which is why she wants to create this book to help parents who want to give the gift of music to their child, but may not have the time or money to do so.

www.ingramcontent.com/pod-product-compliance
Lightning Source LLC
Chambersburg PA
CBHW081249040426
42452CB00015B/2765